HL COHEN

Rutt

Sp...
Su...
Fa...
V...

SCULPTURE
INSIDE AND OUT

SCULPTURE
INSIDE AND OUT

Malvina Hoffman

New York · W · W · NORTON & COMPANY · Publishers

PRINTED IN THE UNITED STATES OF AMERICA

Contents

List of Illustrations

Illustrations of Marble Carving Tools, Page 157; Wood Carving Tools, Page 180; Plaster Tools, Page 257, by Courtesy of Ettl Studios, Inc., New York, from Their Catalogue "Sculpture and Modeling."

Acknowledgment

I SHOULD like to express my thanks and appreciation to those friends and members of my profession who have read the manuscript of the technical chapters and generously given their time and constructive suggestions. Certain master craftsmen in Paris and New York have demonstrated each step of their special process, bronze or marble carving, plaster casting or medal making, with enthusiastic interest. Such professional cooperation, proving how strong and living is the devotion of a good craftsman to his work, has been of invaluable assistance to me.

M. H.

Introduction

So it is impossible to detach the form from
the idea, for the idea only exists by virtue
of the form.   (FLAUBERT)

ALICE went through the looking glass. Lucky Alice! Does not every-one wish to know what goes on behind the looking glass? Is this not perhaps the origin of all our needs of a third dimension? The painter must suggest it to us convincingly by his two-dimensional design, otherwise we find his picture flat and lifeless. This need of depth, which satisfies some fundamental desire of man, may well have been the subconscious force that gave birth to sculpture—something we can touch and feel all around.

Sculpture may be almost anything: a monument, a statue, an old coin, a bas-relief, a portrait bust, a lifelong struggle against heavy odds.

If one of God's children finds he cannot see or feel life in other terms than those of form, if he tries to escape and live outside of this obsession and fails, he generally calls himself a sculptor. Whether he can set the world aglow by his work or not is beside the point. He knows that his daily lot will be a searching for form, it may be in stone, marble, or bronze; it will be a constant analyzing of life itself in terms of three-dimensional silence. But it is certain that if he accepts this yoke of labor he will plow deep under the surface of life, and he will experience miracles and give thanks that he is alive and awake and aware.

Sculpture is a parable in three dimensions, a symbol of a spiritual experience, and a means of conveying truth by concentrating its essence into visible form. Today we call it the interrelation of spatial design, and we look for its quality of volume, light, and shade. It must be the reflection of the artist who creates it and of the era in which he lives, not an echo or a memory of other days and other ways.

If an artist is ready to give his mind and strength to exploring and devouring a subject and to developing his own means of expressing what he has discovered in his searching, his work will not be long ignored.

Integrity and passion have a way of coming through, if they are the forces that drive the sculptor's chisel. Even walls of stone or lumps of metal cannot hold such qualities in oblivion. The finished work will vibrate and be felt even if it is not understood. The artist is responsible only for creating his work, not for the public who may pass it by and feel nothing.

When art is taken as a matter of course, when people grow indifferent, they no longer see the things that surround them. Any port in a calm will do. To change their circulation and startle them into the realization that art is a living, changing force is the artist's mission, and the modern sculptor is contributing his part to this awakening.

Is it the era that makes the artist or the artist who makes the era? Why should there be such a wide gulf between the realm of art and the realm of the religious and scientific searchers of today? Could they not be more closely correlated and mutually understood? The artists, who are seeking for the real essence of form and a totality of thought, may help the world of science and the spirit to find the way towards a universal sensibility and bring our consciousness to a higher plane of evolution. That which "makes nobility in anything is its capacity for enduring." Art recognizes no frontiers or creeds, it is all-inclusive and gives us a feeling of awe in its presence, a new awareness of beauty, a deeper understanding of the meaning of life.

> *Il dépend de celui qui passe*
> *Que je sois tombe ou trésor*
> *Que je parle ou me taise.*
> *Ceci ne tient qu'à toi*
> *Ami, n'entre pas sans désir.**
>
> PAUL VALERY

* It depends on him who passes by
  Whether I am a tomb or a treasure
  Whether I speak or keep silent.
  This rests with you,
  Friend, do not enter without desire.

PART ONE

1. The Egg Itself. (L. MOHOLY-NAGY)

2. Entrance to Eternal Life.

I. Origin of Form

As it was in the beginning . . .

THE bud of the flower, the egg of the animal, the embryo of the human being, eternally repeated, contain the unsolved mystery of life. These symbols of birth represent the origin of form in the great divisions—vegetable, animal, and human.

In recent years we have delved behind many impenetrable walls. Art, science, and mathematics have helped to reveal many secrets which were hidden to past generations, but it is certain that, regardless of progress and modern discovery and invention, the seeker for the origin and cause of things as they are will turn at last to nature for the elemental forces and unchanging wonder of life itself.

In spite of all the thousands of books written on the subject, the phenomenon of birth is still awe-inspiring and veiled in mystery.

The understanding of how we start life in the embryo would reveal to us how microscopic are the inventions of man, in comparison to the intricate and miraculous developments that give form to man before he ever sees the light of day.

If we study the position of the fetus as it appears in about the ninth month of its development we see the tiny body curled up with its head bowed over, the hands crossed, and the knees drawn up to permit the whole structure of bones, muscles, nerves, and arteries to fit comfortably into the cage of the matrix. As it was in the beginning, so it is again at the end of life. Think of the decrepit old human being, bent over, head bowed, seated in a weary, curled-up position exactly similar to the unborn babe's. The cycle of life begins and ends in the same design; only the proportion, size, and shape of the human being change as he passes through the stages of babyhood, youth, maturity, and old age. The eternal oval, the egg itself.

From the earliest records we find frequent recurrences of the egg as the

3. Ātem, First Manifesta-
tion of God in Human Form.

4. Bird with Egg, Easter
Island.

symbol of life in form. The mystery of creation has always been a subject of inspiration to artists. All the great scholars and scientists put together have never been able to contrive anything so marvelous as the combination of spirit and matter in the creation of man.

It has seemed to me that if we are to attempt to understand and interpret man and spend our lives trying to translate our discoveries into a three-dimensional language, it would be wise to start this study at the beginning and find out how we grow into a complete, articulated, and functioning entity. The formation of mind and character is still such a mystery that we are continually baffled by its complexity. I shall only attempt to reveal, through the following illustrations, a few of the most salient steps of mitosis, or cellular division, and its fantastic multiplication which takes place in the formation of a single fertilized egg—the origin of human form.

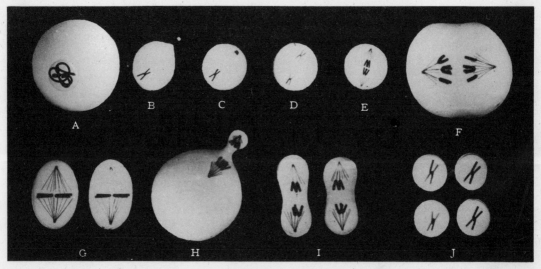

5. A. Immature Sperm Cell. B. Only One Sperm Cell Is Admitted to Fertilization. C. Sper-
matozoon Penetrates Egg Cell. D. Half the Nuclear Mass of Spermatozoon Is Visible Again as
Chromosomes. E. Two Half Nuclei Form Together a Nuclear Spindle, Then Unite as Com-
plete Nucleus. F. Spindle Divides. G. Second Division of Maturing Process Begins. H. Com-
mencing Segmentation of First Polar Cell. I. Chromosomes Do Not Divide; Their Number Is
Halved. J. Second Division Is Ended. (MODERN MUSEUM OF SCIENCE AND INDUSTRY)

II. A Brief Outline of Sculpture

TO attempt to review ever so briefly the vast panorama of sculpture which stretches behind us, we must gird ourselves with patience and fortitude. Our curiosity in the past activities of our fellow men is constant and universal; but this natural desire to know is soon choked or frightened by the endless profusion of material that time and history have accumulated, and more often by the manner in which it is presented.

To select the essentials from the mass and keep your interest alive, I shall condense the material to capsule form, which I confess seems almost an impertinence on my part, in view of the monumental scale of such a subject. To give me courage I must therefore assume that there are those who know less than I do about the history of art, and for this encouraging few I shall try my luck and risk the verdict of the others.

One thinks with awe of the canyons of books on art, tome upon tome written by critics, students, archaeologists, collectors, and sculptors themselves. These books deal with the giants of art who have reappeared through the years, from the nameless prehistoric masters to the yet unclassified "Artist of Tomorrow." They seem to spring from the center of the earth, naked souls, living apart from the world's riches and distractions, and, by some unexplained miracle, living in close contact with elemental forces which endow them with superenergy and wisdom. To these men are attracted the serious students of all time. One turns to them as one turns to the sun, for light, guidance, and well-being.

In spite of all the incorrect information written about various periods and phases of art, something vital always remains if it has ever existed, and we are able to explore by our own means the only free country left to man, where our spirit, mind, and physical powers may all combine their efforts and draw conclusions which are governed by no authority save our own wisdom. We shall develop a scale of values and decide for ourselves which examples of art can stand the test not only of fitting their own era, and being an integral part of it, but which ones embody the qualities that make for universal timelessness. We shall learn not to look for dates or signatures, but for the reflection of beauty and form, and cosmic power.

I suggest that the reader study the illustrations in this chapter thoughtfully, in relation to the times in which they were created, not trying to judge them by standards learned in school, or by the cultural trend of today, but by deselfing himself sufficiently to respond to the message of each outstanding example. They need no word of explanation; they are sufficient and strong enough to make us take off our hats and keep silence before them. It is for the student to absorb the lesson and experience a new capacity for observance and feeling. He must clear his mind of habits of thought and prejudice, and try to live in that blessed state where names, prices, and publicity do not exist.

Understanding and appreciation of art will not come suddenly or even rapidly, but by gradual stages of self-education.

With acquired knowledge and certainty of perception comes a sense of awakening of the mind. It is a joyous and stimulating experience, raising the level of your own intelligence, like discovering treasures hidden in a fog, or climbing altitudes which reveal magnificent new vistas with exciting encouragement to the climber.

Almost all of us are familiar with the Greek tradition and the great names of the fifth and fourth centuries B.C.—Phidias, Praxiteles, Myron, Scopas, Lysippus. It is by these masters that all children are introduced to the great era of art. The perfection of their idealistic sculpture is imbibed by the young quite naturally. I wonder how many of us realize that all the white armies of Greek marble statues with which we are so familiar were originally painted? Would we recognize our old friends in their original colored garb?

The Greco-Roman statues of the Vatican and other museums have been gazed upon by worlds of travelers and carefully starred by endless editions of Baedekers, but perhaps there are still a few facts relating to the early days of art that may be of interest. The reader may be surprised to learn, for instance, that the Cretans used copper for their implements as far back as 3500 B.C., and that it was not until a thousand years later that the Trojans used bronze with an alloy of ten per cent tin and developed the art of casting in Greece and Italy. Decoration on metal was brought in from Egypt and the Orient, and about the sixth century B.C. hollow bronze casting was developed. This naturally gave a great impetus to sculptural ideas. Because of wars and invasions, hundreds of statues were melted down for weapons, but the centuries continued to produce armies of new craftsmen and sculptors to replace the ravages of destruction.

The religious fervor of the thirteenth century in France gave that country the lead in sculptural influence, and her art was imitated by craftsmen of all the other European countries. The great carvings on French cathedrals of this period are as perfect in the upper galleries and unseen corners of the edifice as are the prominent figures that are placed on and beside the entrances. These unknown craftsmen took as much pride in producing and finishing their work as if each detail were to be exhibited and seen by all. What a lesson of noble, conscientious labor these men have left to us!

The Hundred Years' War left its scars on France in the fourteenth century, and Germany advanced in the art of sculpture, while the Flemish artists produced realistic carvings which vividly portray the contemporary life of Flanders rather than exhibiting the spiritual quality of the thirteenth century. English wood carvers developed prodigious skill and craftsmanship.

A wave of realism swept over the fifteenth century, and only in Burgundy did sculpture retain some of its former dignity and monumental character; Germany and Spain developed their rich and intricate decoration to the exclusion of simplicity and architectural form.

In Italy the fifteenth century brought forth great names, such as da Vinci and Pisano, Ghiberti, Donatello, Pollaiuolo, Verrocchio, della Robbia, Mino da Fiesole, Desiderio da Settignano, and Jacopo della Quercia. Many of these men were finished artists in more than one field, and if we study the notebooks of Leonardo da Vinci we are utterly amazed at the scope and indefatigable searching of a single mind.

At the top of this list, and standing unchallenged as the leader of Italian art, is the lonely, tragic, triumphant figure of Michelangelo. His vast knowledge and interpretations of man's struggle and sorrows are eternal in their power and mastery. His art has profoundly influenced Rodin and countless other artists.

Benvenuto Cellini (1500-1571) excelled in decorative and technical skill, exploring the scientific processes of bronze casting. In the same century, Jean Goujon and Germain Pilon contributed outstanding examples of French art.

The casting of bells, an industry in metal dating from the early Middle Ages, expanded enormously. Bells were highly decorated; designs and letters were applied in separate castings. Old bells still ring in Amiens, Beauvais, and Chartres. In 1858 Big Ben, weighing fourteen tons, was cast for Westminster.

In China a catalogue of forty-two volumes was printed in 1751, describing the collection of bronzes in the Pekin palace. A treatise on bronze was written in 1122 B.C. in the Chou dynasty. The beauty of coloring which we find and admire in ancient bronzes is due to oxidation and the fact that many of these pieces have been buried in earth for centuries. The colossal stone sculpture of China and the temple carvings give proof of the Chinese' supremacy in this field.

The baroque style of deep shadows and overdramatic decorative detail and drapery was represented brilliantly by Lorenzo Bernini in Italy; his pupil, Pierre Pujet, worked in France, also Coustou and Pigalle. Clodion continued a more graceful and delicate form of baroque sculpture in France, but we sense the romantic style and miss the grandeur of the ancients.

The eighteenth century produced the great Jean Antoine Houdon, who excelled in portraiture. As a classic interpreter of human character he is unsurpassed; his figures of Diana, Flora, and other subjects are of supreme beauty.

Neoclassicism set the tone for the nineteenth century, but certain brave souls were able to lift themselves out of the tendency of this period. François Rude in France was one of the great and passionate artists who fight ahead of their own times; he produced masterpieces like the group "La Marseillaise" on the Arc de Triomphe, and "Maréchal Ney" at the Observatoire. One seems to hear the cry of his "Marseillaise" echoed in the sculpture of many countries.

Barye broke with tradition by turning to the animal kingdom for inspiration. Another high light was Carpeaux, whose life was a series of struggles and disappointments; yet he triumphed, and created beauty. His group of the dance at the right of the Opera House in Paris is perhaps the best known of his works.

Canova in Italy and Thorwaldsen in Denmark sought to re-create the ideals of antiquity. Alfred Stevens was an important figure in the annals of English art, and in Belgium Constantin Meunier, with his sturdy coal miners and dock laborers, made an important contribution to his country's cultural history. This European list is far too brief, but it may serve as an outline to lead the student up to the present era of art, which took its first revolutionary impetus from Auguste Rodin (Paris, 1840-1917).

The reactionary artists who came after Rodin tried to make sculpture a more impersonal and formal art, though many of them were his pupils and learned some of their lessons from his courage and power of execution, and from the inevitable inspiration which his dynamic and forceful character impressed upon everyone who was privileged to work near him and know him.

Rodin's return to the passionate study of nature caused a great turmoil in the realm of art. Meštrović, the great Yugoslav sculptor, was another powerful influence in the art world at the start of the twentieth century. His daring conceptions reflect the mysticism and poetic tradition of the East. His Slavic racial pride and religious ardor are reflected in most of his work.

Bourdelle, Maillol, Despiau in France, Dobson, Gill, Epstein in England, and hosts of other artists in Russia, Germany, America, lead us through the early years of the twentieth century to the battlefield of contemporary sculpture. Nature, light, and motion—the whole world of vision and perception is being explored from new viewpoints today. Through war and peace, in East and West, no country exists without its inevitable record in art, be it archaic, primitive, classical, romantic, or abstract modern.

6. Statues of Rameses III, Karnak, Egypt.

7. *Statue of the Prince of Judea, Known as "the Statue with Wide Shoulders," in Diorite, Neo-Sumerian Period, About 2400* B.C.

8. *Assyrian Bas-relief, 882-857 B.C., Barracco Museum, Rome.* (ALINARI)

9. *"The Winged Bull," Sculptured Polychrome Brickwork, Assyrian, 5th Century B.C., The Louvre.*

10. "Hera of Samos," First Half of the 6th Century B.C., The Louvre.

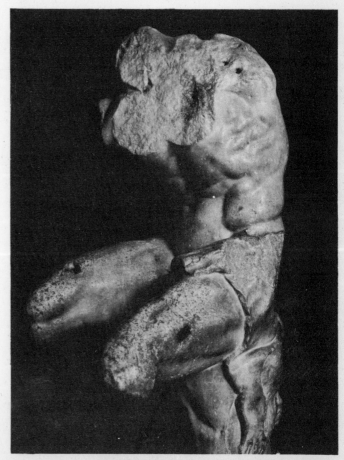

11. Belvedere Torso, Vatican Museum, Rome. (ALINARI)

12. Stone Head from Boro Budur, Java, Museum of Ethnology, Berlin.

13. Bronze Head, Benin, Africa.

14. Colossal Stone Monuments, Easter Island, South Pacific. (EWING GALLOWAY)

15. Marquesan Stilt Steps, Carved Wood, Bishop Museum, Honolulu.

16. *"Calvary," Carved in Granite, Plougastel-Daoulas, Brittany, 1602.*

17. *"Queen of Juda," Stone Carving, 12th Century, Chartres Cathedral.*

36

18. Entrance to the Temple of Sūrya, Konārak, India, Saracenic Sculpture, 13th Century.

19. Twenty-four Stone Monuments on the Road to Shih-san-ling ("Thirteen Tombs") of the Ming Emperors at Chang-ping-chou, China, 15th Century.

20. *"Slave," by Michelangelo, The Louvre.*

38

21. "Maréchal Ney," by François Rude,
Place de L'Observatoire, Paris. (GIRAUDON)

22. Jean Antoine Houdon's Portrait of His
Wife, in Terra Cotta.

23. *Auguste Rodin as a Young Man.*

24. *Antoine Bourdelle and His Head of "La France."*

25. Nude by Aristide Maillol.

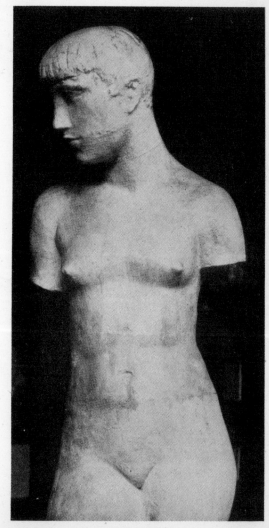

26. Torso by Charles Despiau.

III. *The Timelessness of Art*

Beauty is the primeval phenomenon which itself never makes its appearance, but the reflection of which is visible in a thousand different utterances of the creative mind, and is as various as Nature herself.

(GOETHE)

THE extraordinary modern revolution against the fifth-century B.C. Greek and the "old-fashioned" traditions in art has grown to be universal in its scope. It has included music, painting, sculpture, architecture, literature, drama, and the dance.

No one who wishes to feel himself a living part of the times can ignore the challenge. We may disagree violently as to our taste and judgment concerning modern art, but we cannot afford to side-step the issue. Even the most conservative critics are forced to consider the new attitude of mind and the new rhythms that confront those of us who are awake and alive today.

It is no doubt far easier for those who were born after the beginning of the twentieth century to comprehend and feel themselves in tune with all this self-conscious geometrism and abstraction that pervades the arts.

The favorite adjectives of the nineties must be thrown away into the dustbin. The human side of art is branded as sentimental. Was it a gentler, kinder age that gave birth to the pretty, inoffensive, and rather spineless art of the nineteenth century? Is it science or machinery or psychoanalysis that develops formalism, surrealism, or this aluminum, stream-minded attitude of today?

The whole field of artistic creation is in a state of flux. We have revolted against the past and have jumped into the future, but after all isn't this quite natural? There is no slow or easy way to stop a long habit, except by tearing it out by the roots and facing about in a totally new and opposite direction. The world has a way of turning over in great cycles of evolution and revolution. Lots of little pet ideas and theories are lost in the holocaust and chaos of change, but new ones crop up to take their place, while the fundamental principles of life and art are indestructible and push themselves up above the ashes. They are the phoenix which rises up after the fire has burned away all the unessentials and counterfeits.

Now if we can train our minds to recognize these basic principles, I think we can understand far more intelligently what constitutes enduring qualities in art, regardless of dates or tradition.

Keeping only to sculpture, let us start by considering what was the function of form in the earliest of man's searching for expression. The mystery of life and death, the worship of a higher power, demanded some symbolic form through which man could offer prayers or thanksgiving, or in some way express his conception of the infinite.

The tribal cults began by formulating certain symbolic forms for the worship of the sun, moon, and stars, and later for the more specialized gods. The earliest crude monoliths and stone alignments give their symbolic evidence of such development. The use of form for any personal or individual idea was not thought of in the early periods of man's evolution. The first basic principle of form was cosmic in its meaning; it was the physical link between the consciousness of man and the invisible power of the infinite.

27. Prehistoric Rock Painting of Bison, from the Cave of Altamira, Spain.
(AMERICAN MUSEUM OF NATURAL HISTORY)

28. Colossal Stone Alignments, Carnac, Brittany.

It is quite natural, therefore, that these early stone symbols are gigantic and awe-inspiring. As civilization progressed and the individuality of man became accentuated, the limitless, cosmic significance of form began to recede in scale, and the expression of personal ideas and cultivation of individualism destroyed the grandeur of the elemental period of sculpture.

We have but to visit Carnac in southern Brittany or Stonehenge in England to convince ourselves of the grandeur of the ancients and their stone symbolism used in a cosmic sense.

If we study the work of the Sumerian sculptors of about 2300 B.C. we go far enough back to get a good running start on our own day. The sculptors of that ancient period worked in hard, resisting materials; they had no machines or automatic gadgets to facilitate the grim struggle of man against marble. They conceived their ideas in simple, large forms, and found that by correlating the planes of large masses they could evolve a sort of suggestive symbolism which served to express their ideas in sculpture.

Perhaps they really didn't think about planes at all; perhaps they felt them instinctively (who knows what anyone ever thinks?), but judging their work from today's point of view, they would seem to have solved certain problems in a grand manner which has directly influenced "modern" sculptors, forty-two hundred years later, in both Europe and America.

That is quite a long jump. If now we consider the Egyptian Sphinx and its mysterious secret, and include the pyramids and certain monumental figures, we shall be faced with another challenge: What is it that commands our respect and admiration for these great mountains of stone and granite? They are neither personal nor intimate. Yet they live calmly on through the centuries, unchanged by time or judgment. Let us apply the laws of life and permanent values to these great giants of sculpture; can they stand the test? The cosmic power which they possess comes from their utter rightness in scale and proportion, and in the correlation of their huge surfaces. They have eliminated all unessentials, and have been conceived and executed in correct relation to their purpose and surroundings. Therefore they give us a feeling of being in the presence of eternal majesty.

The simplest forms that suggest themselves to any growing child are the ball, the cube, and the cylinder. The sun was probably the origin of the sphere symbol, the cube may have been the easiest shape to cut in rock with primitive Neanderthal tools, the tree suggests the cylinder. Variations on these forms evolved, and we have the pyramid or pointed cube, dolmens (table rocks) and menhirs (standing rocks) of ancient Brittany. These are the symbolic ancestors of the World's Fair "Sphere and Trylon" of 1939.

It is not difficult to reason out why the primitive African Negro wood carvers are so often influenced by the cylindrical forms of trees. They live in the jungles, they cut the trees and become familiar with their shapes and forms from the earliest days of their awareness. Their vitality and charm lie in this very fact: their wood carvings are the direct echo of their natural instincts and surroundings. They have no preconceived ideas about what sculpture looks like. They have not been taught, but they have felt the meaning and movement of life, and their primitive instincts have symbolized it in wooden images that excite our imagination and teach us drastic lessons. Have we not lost their direct contact with the elemental forces? Who can look at the dramatic little figures from Cameroon or the Gold or Ivory Coast and not feel the thrill that seems to spring out of them? The fact that they often shock the observer by their frank expression of the sex organs is merely a proof of their sincerity. For the power of sex is their tribal pride, and it is not sensuality which they express but the creative force of man.

It is often thought of as a fad, this Negro sculpture. But if we analyze the real cause of its popularity we find that it probably has a sounder reason than is generally attributed to it. Central European sculptors recognized its significance over thirty years ago, and gradually other nations began to discover in this Negro carving the qualities that admit it into the domain of elemental art. Let us hope that the primitive art of our own American Indians may be recognized and given its due place in the annals of American culture. The fine Indian native talent has been too long ignored and classed with exhibits of beadwork and crude silver souvenirs. It is encourag-

29. *African Negro Figurine Carved in Wood.*

30. *Megalithic Monument, Menhir du Champs-Dolent, near Dol, Brittany; 29 Feet Above Ground, 20 Feet Below. The Bretons Have Put a Christian Cross on Its Summit.* (EWING GALLOWAY)

31. *The Great Dolmen, Tregunc, France.*

32. Megalithic Monuments, Stonehenge, Salisbury Plain, England. (EWING GALLOWAY)

ing that at last plans are afoot to build an American Indian Museum in Washington where the best of our national folklore and primitive art will be collected and shown as a living, active force rather than merely as specimens in glass cases.

There have been certain protagonists who, in defending the cause of modern sculpture, have taken rather savage delight in tearing down the idols of the Greek tradition. They have accused the artists of the Parthenon period of dipping their drapery cloths in clay water and hanging them over their lay figures to dry in folds. These, they claim, were in turn copied diligently by stone carvers, and the result is therefore overrealistic, and neither sculptural nor architectural. Perhaps they are right in this last assumption; perhaps the subjects in the Greek pediments do seem a bit far removed from the architectural frames in which they are set. Nevertheless they do radiate beauty, and have given serene enjoyment for centuries.

I cannot quite see why one must attack the dead for the sake of defending the living. Let the sculptors of today strike out for themselves and make their own sparks, or even fires, if they can!

Is it not exciting to be alive in an age of experiment and pioneering? We should all feel the urge to turn over the fresh earth and constantly plant new seeds of thought and action. Nothing is more deadly than the apathy of indifference or self-satisfaction.

The concept of the sculptor of today, it seems to me, is to throw away all the unnecessary details and fancy gestures of the recent past, and swing back into the rhythm of the really ancient tradition. The most extreme examples of modernism are often inspired by the oldest of old masters.

Today the artist is faced with a pretty grim struggle for existence. Quantity has become the god of values, not quality. If an artist can stand up against the odds of today and keep his soul clean and apart from all the temptations of easy jobs and popular ideas, or the alternative of starvation, he will be doing well. He surely has the right to seek his own form of artistic expression if he is ready to suffer for it, and it is true that the honest seeker for form is a lone wolf among the popular artists. His work is generally misunderstood and vituperatively criticized, but he must carry on alone.

It is easy to damn by criticism what we do not thoroughly understand, but it is quite another matter to give a constructive opinion based on a careful and intelligent analysis of a subject. We often hear people say, "Modern artists avoid all the difficulties by hacking great pieces of stone into unrecognizable shapes. Ugliness is everywhere—huge, unwieldy lumps of bodies, square heads, legs like trees, no expression, no beauty. What are they driving at?" But there the layman stops. Does he really try to find out what they are driving at? Does he realize that it is not only in New York or Paris, but all over Europe, Russia, Japan, and China that the present generation of artists is changing the tune of the artistic formula of the nineteenth century?

We are all forced to realize that religion has lost much of its power over man during recent centuries. Man is fighting man all over the earth. The great periods of art have generally coincided with the eras of spiritual renaissance in a people. Today the spirit seems to have been crowded out by man's personal ambition to dominate by force, rather than to seek his salvation by dedication to an ideal.

What will the speed and drama of today's vortex bring forth in the world

33. Equestrian Statue, Polychrome Wood, Schango, Africa, Louis Carré Collection, Paris.

of art? Would it not be stimulating and rewarding to explore and discover just how the artist is meeting his special problem as a barometer of our own time?

Be not too swift to condemn with a careless word the searching of a newcomer. Remember with what derision and scorn many of the great works in sculpture and painting and music were received—works which we have since learned to appreciate and understand.

Let the Sphinx continue to mystify you, but make the effort at least to feel why the best Egyptians, Greeks, and Assyrians, as well as the best in Europe and America today, survive and defy all opposition. If they have built upon permanent and vital laws, if they have captured the illusive secret of form, and light, and transparent shadow, they speak a universal language, and that language is timeless—it is art.

Towards the end of the nineteenth century Rodin was the first to break the rules in Paris. His plastic conceptions were diametrically opposed to those of his predecessors, and his pupils soon gave chase to the old school. He juggled the forms of human bodies into daring movement and unexpected compositions. He experimented with light and shade as freely as he did with form, breaking away from all academic ideas of arrangement. Rodin's marbles express the surging tumult of a soul at grips with life and elemental forces. Always dissatisfied with his own work, and aware of the need of objective simplicity, he was continually torn between passion for human expression and the subconscious knowledge that he was not able to achieve objectivity. To give the synthesis of gesture by a single line, rather than reproduce the actual pose of the model, I have seen Rodin make innumerable drawings, throwing one after the other on the floor and groaning as if in pain (real searching *is* often painful), as he would bow his great shoulders and devour with his eyes the restless play of light and shade on the model. He would say to me, "Never, never can we catch the essence of nature, we are bound like Prometheus to our own limitations! Nature's shadows are transparent, ours seem hard and opaque in their darkness."

After Rodin there followed Bourdelle and Despiau, Brancusi, Gaudier-Brzeska, Gargallo, Zadkine, Epstein, Orloff, and Lipchitz. What a variety of vision and conception is included in just this short list of sculptors! Some of them would drive their chisels directly into mountains of stone, others would polish surfaces until they shone like mirrors; some would bend and hammer great sheets of iron and metal until startling forms would spring into life, others would delve into the mysteries of organic forms and evolve abstract compositions that excite and ensnare us.

There is another group of moderns, known as surrealists, who have included in their field of expression the symbolism and analysis of dreams and unreality. They combine the actual visible world and the subconscious mind in their conception of art. A comparatively small number of this school are sculptors.

Many people condemn the movement of modern sculpture by asking quite casually, "Why should these sculptors feel free to ignore all practical training and jump gaily into the deep end before they have learned to swim?" They do not realize that many so-called moderns have gone through long years of hard technical training, that they are accomplished and expert, and yet have felt so dissatisfied with academic work that they were forced and driven to seek new forms and symbols. Their era drove out the old gods and demanded new ones. They are passionate seekers who are forced by great need to lay out new roads for tomorrow.

Evasion of hard training and craftsmanship is obvious in the senselessness of the work of many sculptors of today. They do not arrive at their abstraction or stylization by normal evolution or sincerity, but by some short cut or abnormal desire to distort form and startle the public, calling attention to their ego by exhibitionism. When, however, abstract art is fresh and stimulating, when it does make sense, because founded on legitimate principles, the result excites our imagination and opens vistas of thought and perception. A new simplicity is far more difficult to achieve than accepted complexities.

It is good to know that the sculptors of our time are searching for a new idiom. When the abstract or modern artist gives us a direct and brave conception of spatial design, with unexpected angles of balance, or play of light and shade, we should be thankful instead of scornful. We learn to detect living patterns of movement and our minds are shaken out of old habits.

In July, 1914, I had the privilege of helping Rodin in the sorting and classification of his drawings at the Hôtel Biron (now the Musée Rodin). Earlier in the same month he had asked me to direct the installation of his great exhibit of bronzes and marbles at Grosvenor House, London. Later, when we were working together at the Biron one day the concierge came in and in ominous, hoarse tones announced that war was declared; that was August 2, 1914. I shall never forget Rodin's remark at that moment, "Oh, la civilisation . . . la civilisation des hommes. . . . C'est une mauvaise couche de peinture qui s'en va quand la pluie tombe!" *

* Oh, civilization—the civilization of man! It's a bad coat of paint that comes off when it rains.

Twenty-four years later, in the autumn of 1938, there came another day of world anxiety, with all Europe holding its breath in dread anticipation of what the Dictator of Germany might decide to do. Awaiting his radio broadcast, it seemed as if the destiny of the world were hanging in the balance. On this day I spent two most illuminating hours with the father of modernism in its abstract, universal sense, Constantin Brancusi. In spite of the fact that he was on the eve of leaving for Rumania, and that the world was in a state of indescribable tension, he answered my knock at his door, and received me, a stranger, with calm and smiling cordiality, in his picturesque and typical studio "au fond de la cour" in the celebrated Impasse Ronsin, in Paris.

Brancusi was born in Rumania in 1876. He has consistently clung to his own passionate conviction that a work of plastic art must have beauty and rhythm, and be a complete composition from every point of view. To achieve this, he told me, he had explored every technical road to training to its extreme limit. When he had perfected his skill in clay modeling and drawing, and had made a complete anatomical figure to anchor his knowledge of human anatomy, he began to feel a great unrest in his mind.

He searched and experimented in all directions, making endless studies of the figure and numberless portraits. He said, while he looked for photographs of his early works, "When a sculptor reaches a point of virtuosity in his direction, and can surpass his rivals in translating reality into forms, he reaches an impasse." He spread out the photographs of his realistic period. "I craved for limitless horizons, while I was carving a great group into stone, and when it was completed I was utterly convinced that all my efforts and training had proved just one thing; I was sure that I had thoroughly explored certain roads and they could yield me no further spiritual experience." This struck me as a significant and revealing statement.

He then made his decision to bury his past in his subconscious mind, and start forth on new worlds of discovery.

At this point he led me to the various interpretations of the well-known Mlle. Pogany. "You see," he said musingly, "this was the first idea." The hands were modeled quite definitely, the hair bound into a coil at the back of the head; but the face had been generalized almost to the extent of obliteration of the features, except for the eyes and arching sweep of the eyebrows. In the next version, the head became the oval form of the final version; in the next the two hands and arms had become one inclusive form, and the hair was lower on the neck and treated as a design of flowing curves. In the final version (but is anything final?) the head, hands, and hair all flow together in unison. The curves sweep up from the base like a growing plant, enveloping the neck and giving their theme to the whole composition. There is unquestionably a sequence of evolution here that can defy what anyone else thinks. The artist has depersonified himself and his subject, and has evolved a plastic symbol which arrests and suggests new vistas of thought. The polished brass surface is one experiment, the polished marble another. "Perhaps I may think of still a better interpretation some day," he said, as he turned the head over and over in his hands. "Who can ever say that a work of art is finished?"

As we wandered about the studio, finding our way between blocks of marble and gigantic plaster columns of strange, exotic shapes, Brancusi suddenly said, "You remember the story in mythology, when a god was changed into a swan and Leda fell in love with this bird?" His face had grown suddenly young and his eyes were smiling like a mischievous child. He leaned over and plugged a wire into a wall outlet. "Well," he whispered, "I never believed it!" A strange brass form, poised on a revolving disk, began to turn around slowly, almost imperceptibly, before us, reflecting on its mirrorlike surface all the objects in the studio and ourselves in melting, changing lights and shades. "You see," said Brancusi, "I never could imagine a male being turned into a swan, impossible, but a woman, yes, quite easily. Can you recognize her in this bird?" I looked more carefully as he drew his finger along the outline, saying, "She is kneeling, bent backwards. Can you see now? These high lights were her breasts, her head . . . but they were transformed into these bird forms. As they turn they are forever transforming into new life, new rhythm . . . do you feel it?" The luminous mythological bird kept on turning, its abstract surface reflecting in silent, continuous motion the kaleidoscopic patterns on the glassy surface of the metallic mirror below.

The daylight faded in the white studio, and I became conscious of the deepening shadows. Brancusi moved slowly about the studio in his white blouse and wooden sabots, from time to time running his fingers through his thick white hair. He lifted the dustcloths off the other work, revealing the flossy veined surfaces of his great, flat marble fish poised on a single pivoting point. Pushing this gently at one end, he said as it gained momentum, "When you see a fish, you do not think of its scales, do you? You think of its speed, its floating, flashing body seen through water. . . . Well, I've tried to express just that. If I made fins and eyes and scales, I would arrest its movement and hold you by a pattern, or a shape of reality. I want just the flash of its spirit. Do you understand me now?" I did.

The impeccable craftsmanship drew my admiration, the sense of inevitable balance and proportion fascinated me. Everything seemed to be poised in space, lightly, ready to fly or swim or turn without effort. Here indeed one feels the result of a life struggle to capture and reveal the secrets of natural phenomena.

"Sculpture must be lovely to touch," he said, "friendly to live with, not only well made . . . fancy living with Moses, by Michelangelo, even if we do acknowledge and admire his power! We should not be made to feel like atoms in its presence, but we should vibrate and respond to the miracles of life. What is so glorious as the privilege that man enjoys of being alive, and being able to see and discover beauty all about him! Nature creates plants that grow up straight and strong from the ground; here is my column, it is in the beautiful garden of my friend in Rumania. Its forms are the same from the ground to the top, it has no need of pedestal or base to support it, the wind will not destroy it, it stands by its own strength, like . . . ," he hesitated, "like a giant cactus in our California deserts," I added. "Yes," he said, "that is so. In a few days I hope to see this installed in Rumania; it is thirty meters high and you know that my friend there once told me that he had never been aware of the great beauty of his garden until he had placed my column there, it had opened his eyes . . . that is what we artists are here for . . . to reveal beauty. This studio is my garden; here I am alone, and happy. Today, outside in the city, all is confusion and distress, the black wings of war are hovering over Europe."

I rose to take my leave, and asked if I might have a photograph of his most recent work for this little book I had written on sculpture. Noticing a group of high-powered spotlights in a corner of the studio and a great camera on a tripod, I asked if he did all his own photography. "Yes, always . . . and moving pictures also, here is my laboratory, and here are my pictures of the Temple du Baiser. You may have them for your book, they are recent ones. Tomorrow I shall go to see this gateway inaugurated in my country. Through this doorway one will enter a garden. . . . Do you recognize the patterns on the stone? Here are the plaster models of the supporting columns; what do you see in them?" I thought for a few moments. "I see the forms of two cells that meet and create life . . . like the revelation I once saw through a microscope when I studied embryology. The beginning of life . . . through love. Am I right?" "Yes, you are," he answered, "and these columns are the result of years of searching. First came this group of two interlaced, seated figures in stone . . . then the symbol of the egg, then the thought grew into this gateway to a beyond . . . and now I shall develop these figures in the pattern above the gateway. Do you recognize them?" I did.

Looking at the piles of drawings and photographs he had scattered all over the studio, searching for those which he wished to show to me, I felt guilty and offered to pack them for him. "Oh, it is nothing," he said. "My valises will soon be ready. I am used to all this sort of thing." I could not help saying, "It is curious how the busiest great artists always find time to help others along the way.

"I must go now, Mr. Brancusi, it is late and you have given me so many new visions, new wings to my imagination. You are going to Rumania, and I am going to America; who knows, what may come next? When your two symbols met they created a gateway to a garden beyond; perhaps our thoughts too may have met, and there will be another flower born in the garden."

I walked away slowly; Paris was in complete darkness; only a dim blue light marked the corners of the streets, and the air was heavy with oppression and silence. Suddenly the rising whistle of a practicing air-raid siren began to climb into a shrill scream of warning, tearing the silence to shreds. A shiver ran down my spine. I stopped and looked at a group of workmen and taxi drivers sitting at their sidewalk café. One of them caught my eye, and shrugging his shoulders called out, "Don't worry, little lady, it's only a dress rehearsal in case . . ." He was not far from the truth.

34. *Paul Dardé, the Sculptor, in the Roman Doorway He Has Reconstructed on His Estate at Saint-Maurice, Hérault, France.*

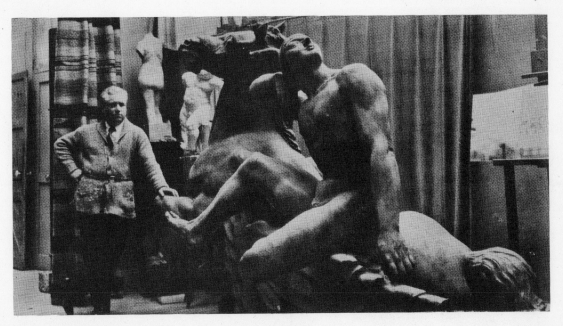

35. *Alfred Auguste Janniot in His Studio, Paris.*

36. *Head of Bullfighter, in Iron, by Pablo Gargallo.*

37. *"Don Quixote," in Bronze, by Marie-Louise Simard, Luxembourg Museum.*

38. Eric Gill, Standing Beside His Bas-relief for the Palace of the Nations, Geneva. (HOWARD COSTER)

39. "Ceres," by Gilbert Ledward, Life-size Stone Figure.

58

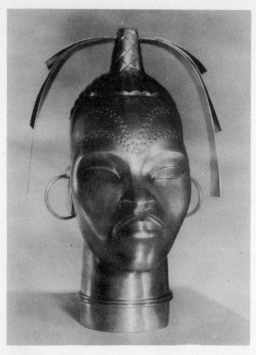

40. "African Warrior," in Brass, by Hazel Armour.

41. "Grief," by Georg Kolbe, Collection of Mr. and Mrs. Erich Cohn, New York. (MUSEUM OF MODERN ART)

42. "Nijinsky," in The Carnival *of Schumann, by E. O. de Rosales, Collection of Lionberger Davis, St. Louis.*

43. "The Boxer," by the Italian Sculptor, Francesco Messina.

44. Polychrome Sculpture by Arturo Martini, Palace of Justice, Milan.

45. *Stone Sculpture by Ossip Zadkine.*

46. *Wood Carving by Gustave Miklos, Greek Sculptor.*

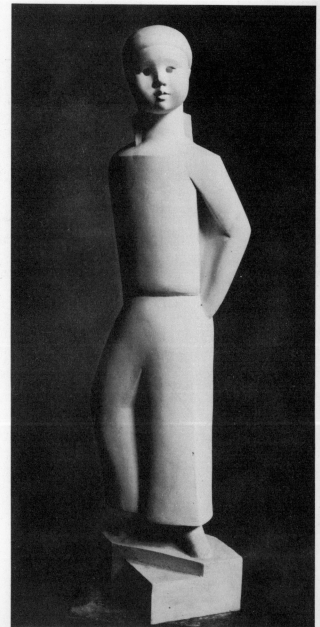

47. *Sculpture by Jacques Lipchitz.*
("LIPCHITZ," BY MAURICE RAYNAL)

48. *"My Son," by Chana Orloff, in Cement, Grenoble Museum.* (MARC VAUX)

49. "Europa and the Bull," by Carl Milles. (WORCESTER ART MUSEUM)

12/930 Oslo. Abel-monumentet.

50. *"Abel," by Gustav Vigeland, Oslo.*

51. *"Heracles and the Hydra," by Rudolph Tegner, Copenhagen.* (VIZZAVONA)

52. "*Dancing Girl,*" *by William Zorach, in Aluminum, at the Radio City Music Hall, New York.*

53. "*The Prisoner,*" *by Ramón Mateu, Spanish Sculptor.*

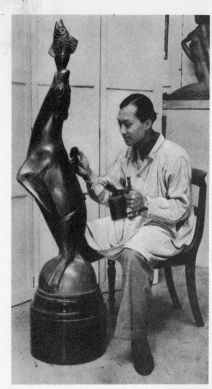

54. *Prince Birabongse Bhamnbandi of Siam, Patining "Sea-lion Swallowing Fish."* (THE "BYSTANDER," LONDON)

55. *"The Two Natures of Man," by George Gray Barnard, Metropolitan Museum.*

56. "Armillary Sphere," by Paul Manship. (DE WITT WARD)

57. *"The Struggle of Elemental Man," by Malvina Hoffman, Front View.* (PHOTO BY M. H.)

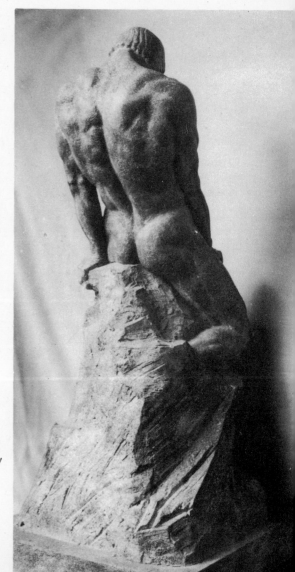

58. *"The Struggle of Elemental Man," by Malvina Hoffman, Back View.* (PHOTO BY M. H.)

59, 60, 61. *Sculpture by Constantin Brancusi. "Temple of the Kiss." Note the Figure Group Theme in the Bas-relief at the Top. Group of Figures. "Temple of the Kiss" as it Appears at the Gateway to the Public Garden in Targu Jiu, Rumania, Showing Round Stone Table and Seats.* (PHOTO BY BRANCUSI)

62. *"Leda," Polished Bronze, by Brancusi.*

63. "My Mother," by Ivan Meštrović, Chicago Art Institute.

IV. "Having Eyes, See Ye Not?" *

WE all have eyes, but how many of us use them really to see and study the panorama of life that spreads its wonders before us? We look at everything, we even gaze fondly at those we love, but do we often try to transfer this image to our memory by a conscious act of keen observation? Perhaps the more we love the less we see—hence, "Love is blind."

If we do not connect our vision with our mind, we merely direct the lenses of our camera and forget to open the shutter which will instantly record on a sensitive plate the impression of light and shape of that which is exposed to the lens.

"Having eyes, see ye not?" Does this not apply to many of us? In most of the human race there is a careless indifference to the priceless possession of two good eyes. Perhaps it is the consciousness of this treasure that some-times overcomes an individual and makes him an artist—who knows? Cer-tainly artists use and appreciate their eyes with more passionate intensity than most people. They spend their lives endeavoring to register visual im-pressions, and transfer them to their memory or mental storehouse, from which they may draw information for years to come; then also, there is that "inward eye, which is the bliss of solitude."

To those who have been deprived of their eyesight, it is often given that their "inward eye" becomes an astounding and supersensitive possession. We are often amazed by the way blind people can record a vivid impression by the training and sensitizing of all their other faculties. It is by years of agonizing concentration that they generally achieve this phenomenal inner vision—by the constant effort to co-ordinate all their other senses in the struggle to replace their outward vision. They learn to measure distance

* Mark viii, 18: "Having eyes, see ye not? And having ears, hear ye not? And do ye not remember?"

72

by the number of steps, or by the reach of an arm or length of a finger. They train their sense of touch to a point of accuracy that would shame anyone whose eyesight is perfect. I have seen a blind man build a ground plan and elevation of a modern house by sticking matches to a sheet of compoboard. By touching these raised lines he could visualize accurately the proportions of walls, windows, and doorways; by bending wires he could design curves; and by studying a bas-relief in hard wax through his finger tips, he could direct the carving of wooden ornament and the casting of every detail such as doorknobs, handrails, bases for lamps, etc. It is true that this phenomenal man, Jean Julien Lemordant, who was blinded in the war, had been trained as an architect, and had studied draftsmanship and painting to a point where his talent had already expressed itself in fine pictures and mural decorations. The tragedy of losing his eyesight was a more poignant agony because of this very fact. He had used his eyes not only to look at life, but to search it to its very heart.

Not long ago I had a visit from Helen Keller. She is another of those brave souls who have shown the world that the spirit can overcome physical handicap, that the mind can focus on the development of sensitivity as a means to understanding life. In the place of sight and speech and hearing, she has built herself a fortress of insight, a finger language of touch, and a listening heart that not only can register the outer aspect of life, but which senses that mysterious psychic vibration which emanates from within. She responds with an instantaneous reaction more vivid than the superficial and often casual utterances of human speech.

When Miss Keller entered the studio she knew at once that she was in a high-ceilinged, vast space. By her own mysterious awareness, she soon began to understand the meaning of the various figures and reliefs that her fingers stroked. They rippled over the surfaces, swiftly following the outlines and curves of the general contours; then she would find the head and stop, slowly touching the brow and eyes, gauging the line of the profile and the width of the bony structure; then, with extraordinary delicacy, she would follow every detail of expression—the eyes, nose, and lips would be analyzed in silence. Suddenly she would start and smile and by her hand language reveal to us that she had discovered the subject, a Cambodian girl dancing on the seven-headed cobra, the unmistakable curve of the dancer's fingers, turned backward. "How far, how far?" she wondered. "They almost touch the back of the wrists—how wonderful!" And then we led her to a heroic-sized portrait.

Her sympathetic companion held Miss Keller's hand and interpreted by the touch of her fingers what others said in words, and what Miss Keller wished to express. We did not say who the subject was. Miss Keller examined every detail: head, hair, face, and shoulders. Suddenly her fingers caught the furrows in his brow. "This man is deeply troubled; he is not in his own world . . . he is trying to solve a terrible problem—wait." Her fingers traced the contours of eyes and cheekbones. "Slavic type, yes, powerful, deep-set eyes, but they are weary, downcast. He is in deep meditation—a great soul in distress. I begin to know him. Yes, yes—but here on the shoulders, are these wings folded?" I answered, "Yes, they are the wings of an eagle, his country's symbol." Her fingers found the raised inscription on the pedestal. "Oh," she cried, "of course. This is the great Paderewski, who fought so gallantly for his Poland in that strange country of politics, which was so far from his world of music. Yes, I can feel his sorrow, his struggles. There is only one great Paderewski forever. . . ."

Then we led her to a life-sized, draped figure of a man. Her fingers immediately discovered the folds of drapery and the rope girdle. She stooped quickly and verified her impression by tracing the sandals on his feet. "A monk," she signaled to her companion's hand—"but wait. I find a wolf pressing his head closely to the side of this man. Here is a rabbit tucked into his arm, and higher up there is a bird nestled into the fold of his cowl, which falls back. Yes, his head is raised to the sky, his lips are praying. It seems to me he is saying: Little brothers, do not fear; we are friends. . . ." Miss Keller started suddenly and her face became illuminated. "Oh," she cried, "it is St. Francis and his friends, the animals. . . ."

Could anything prove more dramatically the wonder of the inner vision, and the power of the mind over physical handicaps? This experience will always live in my memory. It was a complete revelation to me, like discovering a sixth sense—a sort of direct current between the world of form and the world of the mind.

"The Eye should concentrate, devour; the brain formulate . . . ," said Cézanne.

It is always surprising to realize how seldom any of us are taught how to use our eyes. Even in reading we seldom recognize that in skimming over the printed page we should not merely use our eyes to see the words, but that we should establish an automatic connection between them and our mental storehouse. How many of us try to commit to memory a sentence, two or three words, or even the thought of what we are reading? When we see some garden or house of exceptional beauty or interest, do we make any sustained effort to memorize just what has made the impression? Can we describe the approximate proportions or colors, the distances between paths and flower beds? Could we draw the position of the various pieces of furniture, or identify the colors of carpets and hangings? The powers of the human mind are infinitely more diverse and profound than we realize. The fact is that most of us are mentally lazy, or have been taught too casually how to enjoy our senses without any intense effort.

We miss worlds of experience, as a result of this, and when the need arises, and we wish to use or refer to something we have seen and enjoyed, we find our mental storehouse has retained only indefinite and rather dusty impressions.

A great deal depends on the manner in which children are taught to read and write and observe the infinite, changing wonderland in which we live. Interest is soon aroused if their imagination and curiosity are tapped, and if a subject is presented as a living, active part of their own experience, and not, as is so often the case, as something to be learned and then put away on a shelf to be forgotten with schoolbooks and examination marks. And this applies to adults, as well. Why do they not continue the thrill of discovery all their lives? Certain it is that there is plenty to explore, and wonders yet unknown to be drawn out of the great well of wisdom.

The simple words of Confucius give pause for thought in this day of hurry and noise and jitters. "Is it not pleasant to learn with a constant perseverance and application . . . ? I do not open up the Truth to one who is not eager to get knowledge, nor help out anyone who is not anxious to explain himself. When I have presented one corner of a subject to anyone, and he cannot from it learn the other three, I do not repeat my lesson. . . ."

We often hear the primitive tribes of Africa and the South Seas, or our own American Indians, spoken of as untaught savages. The truth is that from their infancy these people are taught to use their senses and faculties far better than the children of the so-called higher civilized peoples.

Book learning is, of course, not in their line; calendrical examinations and yearly reports do not bother them, but the youngsters of a tribe are watched so constantly by their elders that every day is an examination day. Their skill and their eye are trained from infancy; their strength, balance, and sense of direction and proportion must be sure and accurate. Their life depends on this, and here we have the reason why so much good art, design, and craftsmanship are found among them.

What a pity that the youngsters in our cities cannot be made to know and feel that their life depends on these things too; that proportion and scale, and strength and eye are all part of our vital equipment.

An Indian will never forget a trail that he has once followed. His eye automatically commits to his memory the direction of the streams, the silhouettes of mountains or valleys. This instinct for line and color is ready at a moment's need. Give a young Indian boy a pot of paint and a brush, and watch him decorate a wall. No art school, no teaching of methods and styles. The subconscious security of knowledge is there to be drawn upon. The design flows from the brush naturally. Animals, trees, mountains are in the mind, alive, ready to spring out and express themselves in their own vitality and style.

In Bali boys of twelve to sixteen years carve more expertly than our art academy graduates. They begin when their senses awaken to the life about them, and they are made to realize that this observation and knowledge of visible form and color constitute an integral part of life. It is not labeled as "art" nor taken up as either a pastime or a fad, or as a short period of extreme cramming for collegiate credits.

"The study of art" is an all-inclusive sort of term. Generally it is thought of as meaning drawing, modeling, or painting, but in stark reality it should mean the study of life, for what goes on about us, or within us, is the stuff that art is made of. When we have the rare good fortune to meet a really great artist we generally realize that what makes him great is not only the work of his hands but the depth and dynamic force of his mind and spirit. We find a superman who has torn away the veils of life, seen behind the walls of reality and tragedy, and penetrated into the wilderness where dwells the primitive savage, the instinct of wild beasts; a man who has listened to the silences of the night, and heard the whispers of the dark forest and the song of the secret bird. These giants who have wrestled with their souls, and fought devils, and been on speaking terms with angels, are men of profound wisdom and humility before the wonders of God and nature.

Art includes not only the visible, but also the invisible world—the power of thought to crystallize and draw out the very essence of what constitutes our own era. An artist must be fearlessly a prophet of his own times. If his spirit revolts against rules and traditions, he must be brave enough to strike out alone and break down the protective habits of accepted formula. He must be ready to go ahead alone, without praise or understanding or encouragement. If he is true to himself, his own soul will be his guide, philosopher, and friend. If he needs more than his own conviction of truth, he is lost.

Such a challenge generally weeds out the majority of aspirants. The list of great artists is not so long that one need fear any overcrowding or housing problems on Parnassus.

V. Can Sculpture Be Taught?

In the elder days of art
Builders wrought with greatest care
Each minute and unseen part
For the Gods see everywhere.
(LONGFELLOW)

SCULPTURE cannot be taught by books or the spoken word; it must be experienced by the artist. Art is a command. The hands must be trained by practice, the mind by constant acquisition of knowledge, and the heart by its undefeated faith and desire to overcome all obstacles. For sculpture is a thorny road beset by barriers, defeats, and disappointments.

Art is, however, made of the stuff that dreams are made of, and they say the dreamer is a favorite of the gods. To him they whisper their secrets, to him the moon reveals her innermost beauty, and the night will enfold him to her heart and guard him with her strong dark wings.

The poet and the artist must be ready to harness Pegasus to pull a heavy load. Labor and fatigue are the inevitable price of accomplishment, for no great creation is easily conceived or expressed. Art has been called the Holy Land where the initiates seek to reveal the spirituality of matter.

For grownups as well as for children the intelligent study of art can be of great benefit. Psychologists and physicians agree that manual labor helps to readjust the mind to a balanced rhythm. The training of the hands to respond deftly to the mind is a distinct and joyful experience. When the skill of an artist becomes that of an expert, the creator may sense a sort of ecstasy in the actual accomplishment of a difficult task.

Even though we generally fall far short of our aim, we still are impelled by this ever-flowing stream of hope and desire to try again to surpass ourselves. Failures are many and often devastating to our morale, but one or two bull's-eye successes will carry us over months of hard labor. No composer would attempt to write a musical composition until he had studied the theory and technique of his art, harmony, counterpoint, and orchestration. No sculptor can hope to create a work of art without the equipment of a thorough knowledge of his craft.

A real artist cannot be encouraged or discouraged. He will overcome all obstacles to gain his objective. He will be his own severest critic and come up from any beating with renewed faith and determination. He will not wait for inspiration: he will search passionately and work ceaselessly, finding his inspiration reborn in every problem that he tackles.

When someone asks me cheerfully if I think they could "take it up" as a pastime, I generally suggest social service as a less severe occupation—or travel. The idea of what sculpture really entails comes as a complete blow to most people. Their curiosity has led them to ask, "How do you make a bronze?" and as the answer is a long and complicated one, they generally change the subject before they are obliged to concentrate too painfully. Sometimes they ask if their talented child should go to Paris to study, or if art could be learned in America. A typical case would be the following:

"My girl is eighteen, just out of school, doesn't like parties, has done a great deal of modeling and drawing, has never studied with any teacher, intends to devote all her time to art. We think she is very talented, what can you suggest?"

SCULPTOR: "Bring me what your child has done and let me see everything, drawings, models, sketches, and above all let me observe and question the student alone."

STUDENT: "Oh, I've only modeled one head, and these drawings are from casts, these others are portraits of my friends; of course they are just sketches."

SCULPTOR: "Is this all you have done?"

STUDENT: "Yes, and I've never taken any lessons from anybody; I want to go to Paris. Please tell my father I should be sent over there."

SCULPTOR: "Do you wish to amuse yourself in art, or learn what it really means?"

STUDENT: "Oh, I want to draw and model and keep my mind busy. I want to do something."

SCULPTOR: "I wonder if you can understand what I mean if I quote you four lines of a poem which I think sums up a work of art in sculpture, just as well as it describes the essence of a poem.

A poem should be equal to
Not true

.   .   .

A poem should not mean
But be." *

If the student shows an intelligent reaction, there is hope, if not . . . well, there are many other roads that could be suggested, rather than encouraging her to attempt sculpture.

In most cases the ideal plan to challenge a young hopeful (and they are legion) would be to send him or her to a practical school of technical training (if one exists) where the pupils are taught how to drive a nail straight, or saw a plank, miter a few corners, and plane the surface of rough wood until the hands become used to holding and directing tools. After this introduction they should be taught how to bend and twist wires. They should learn to cut pipes with metal saws, fit them together, and attach lead pipe into sufficient armatures to hold clay in place. Let the pupil build up an idea in clay and learn how to cast it in plaster. The student will soon show ability or lack of it, tenacity of purpose or lack of sincerity and interest. All this may seem unnecessary to the beginner, *but it is not!* These first low jumps are just tryouts.

A student often feels that after a certain period of study he will suddenly become an artist, whereas if he is really an artist both at heart and in his spirit, he knows that he will never reach his ideal and that he will remain a humble student to the end of his days. The mirage of beauty leads him forward along lonely and exhausting roads, and at the end of each journey he knows that the mirage is no nearer, only the light has broken through more vividly and his faith is stronger than ever, that the struggle is worth while, and that no passionate effort is ever wasted.

The artist records the spiritual history of his time. His work lives on to tell the future generations the inner workings of man's conscious and subconscious mind; be it realistic or abstract, nonobjective or cubistic, it is still a record of evolution or revolution, a soaring of wings or a slipping downward, and this responsibility must be accepted and revered.

New ideas and new methods may all be very well, but the old idea of learning your job thoroughly has never been improved upon. "Whatever may change, Art remains what it was two thousand years ago, and two

* Archibald MacLeish.

thousand years hence it will be in all its principles and in all its great effects upon the mind of man, just the same" (RUSKIN).

Transitions of approach to an old subject are always difficult and slow in process. But America is certainly facing the fact that the twentieth century demands a new outlook on the problems of training the young, housing them, and understanding them.

There have been many constructive experiments tried out in the field of the arts, and every year these battlefields of opinions and criticisms find the necessity to change and readjust themselves to the demands of the day. The faculty endeavors to find the best way for the students, while the students inevitably decide that the methods are wrong and that they could all evolve something better. The only slip is: Do they? A good deal of time is spent in finding fault rather than actually suggesting constructive improvements.

Surely the amount of time and money spent in art education is enormous. Think of the installation and work involved at Cranbrook, near Detroit, where leaders in architecture, sculpture, painting, weaving, and other arts and crafts spend their lives directing and inspiring those who are lucky enough to absorb and profit by their experience.

Bennington College is another teeming, active center of art methods. The Tyler School of Fine Arts, connected with Temple University, in Philadelphia, reveals what can be done to train the art student, not only in the theory, but in every practical working phase of the arts and crafts. There the student must model, draw, and carve his way through the first years of learning. The painter must grind his own colors and prepare his own canvases. The sculptor must cast his own plaster, and carve his wood and stone; then he learns the processes of bronze casting, both by sand and by lost-wax methods, the chasing and patining of his finished work. As wisely stated by the Director, Mr. Boris Blai: "Experience is knowledge. To accept the opinion of others without personal awareness is ignorance, waste, and imitation."

This practical-demonstration method is certainly the best and should be the one to be encouraged throughout the land. The days of guilds and apprentices are over, but the need is still here for expert craftsmen who take pride and pleasure in doing their work superlatively well.

The public should realize that nothing would contribute more to the beauty and culture of their country than to aid in the development of a teaching center of this type. Art need no longer be thought of as a specialized study, mysteriously disguised by all the "isms" and "ists" as a means of spending time harmlessly. It is time to awake and demand the right sort of training. Whether it be a handmade tool or a public monument, it should be given the best that any of us have, to endow it with strength and beauty.

It is gratifying to read in the New York *Times* of June 28, 1938, that art appreciation is at last considered a basic need, and that art experience is indispensable to the production of a decent society. The article states that college professors have at last become convinced that education should begin with art, for the sake of a balanced, orderly mind, and that the culture received through art will develop the individual, because a true artist is a leader in reconstruction of personal outlooks and ways of living. Dr. Lester Dix, of Lincoln School, Teachers College, went so far as to declare that "art is a great expander and enricher of experience. It rounds out and matures the meanings of experience, and he who has felt this will not willingly go back to a thinner existence."

I have known frequent examples of people who, having suffered a mental upheaval or long illness from nerves, have turned to the serious study of art with extraordinary benefit. Their minds are directed in new channels of thought, they become aware of their hands and eyes as never before; the feeling of actually modeling in clay or carving wood has filled them with a new curiosity and enthusiasm.

Regardless of circumstance or age, we all have need of some sort of creative occupation. It is this deep, fundamental urge to make something tangible that lurks in the background of many a sick mind. The individual may not be aware of what is causing a certain hunger or dissatisfaction with life, but more often than not it is the lack of an outlet for just this creative instinct.

Back in the earliest days of art our primitive ancestors worked out their excess energies and nervous dynamics in hunting and fighting. We city dwellers are so bound up in our canyons of brick and machinery that we ignore many of the normal needs of our human mechanism.

The sincere, thinking artist is automatically something of a psychologist. His materials are nature, man, and the world of the spirit. He must continually try to penetrate into the deeper consciousness of life and sensitize himself to feel and understand the underlying principles of nature and man's behavior. Sculpture can include the formation and direction of personality as well as plastic expression of ideas.

It is certain that when students are young and full of boundless energy, it is difficult to slow them down to a continuous, concentrated study of any one subject. Their minds spring ahead to new ideas, and their curiosity drives them to explore everything superficially rather than profoundly; but it is also true that the young mind assimilates more rapidly when it does study than the adult mind, except in unusual cases. For this reason a would-be artist should begin to draw and observe everything about him at an early age, and if he has the real fire he will do this without urging. In fact, it will generally be such a constant activity that it will interfere with his other school studies. A wise teacher will try to understand his pupil's greatest interest and with sympathetic counsel will help him to divide his time satisfactorily; the young artist will respond to this guidance of understanding with gratitude.

Many well-known sculptors and painters are utterly incapable of teaching others. They can create art, but remain inarticulate about its methods and technique. Sometimes a great sculptor, although unable to express his art coherently in words, may exert such a powerful influence by his own achievements and character that the pupils derive great benefit from visits to his studio, and the feeling that perhaps some day they may be able to create something that will bring them a word of approval from the master whom they admire as a personality and respect as an artist.

If they study their technical problems with another teacher, and train their hands to obey their minds, they may profit incalculably from an occasional visit and talk with their inarticulate master; but alas, many pupils rely too much on just the glamour of such association, and neglect the more arduous task of studying anatomy, drawing, and the endless challenges of modeling from life. Sooner or later the moment will come when they will have to learn the rules of the game, and the sooner they find this out the better for them and for their art.

There are many brilliant teachers who have the rare gift of guiding and leading others to their distant goal. But there are also, unfortunately, many less gifted who pass on only what they have read in books rather than what they have themselves experienced. It is discouraging to think of the thousands of hours spent by pupils diligently trying to follow mistaken methods of teaching art. After years of effort, they realize they are not progressing or improving; they grow stale and keep repeating their mistakes. If the light breaks through by itself, or if some honest and able critic tells them they are on the wrong track, they should throw off all their habits of error, go to a completely different teacher and environment, and lose no time in starting all over again from the *beginning*.

This means learning to *draw*, not to sketch cleverly or make pretty pictures that will be admired. It means drawing from nude models and redrawing these models from memory, not only copying what the eye sees, but expressing the line of motion and masses of forms and direction of planes. Study the main structure of the body, and familiarize the eye with different sizes and scales of drawings; shift the position from which the model is seen so that the pose becomes an all-around composition, not only a one-view design; squat on the floor and look up from below—the whole impression is new and a fresh set of problems present themselves; climb up a ladder and draw from above.

Imagine what we all look like to our dogs! The effect of foreshortening must be alarming. By the way, how many of us know that dogs see no color, only shades of black, gray, and white? Think of making a correct drawing of a dinner party from Fido's point of view. But why not?

I recall how frequently Rodin would suggest lighting a candle and walking around some beautiful Greek or Egyptian marble. The continuous, flowing forms could stand this "acid test," but a piece of mediocre sculpture would fall to pieces and show up all its sharp defects of construction and the relative values of light and shade, so beautifully balanced and understood by the great old masters.

"Do not be afraid of realism," Rodin often said to me. "To understand nature is a lifelong study." You must add yourself to what you see, and infuse the object with the passionate essence of your own thought; then the result will be not merely realistic, but it will be the merging of matter and spirit. The majesty of the mountain will be transmuted by the inner vision, and its beauty distilled and vitalized. To arrive at these heights, however, the artist must go apart and fight alone. He must needs create his own isolation and resist all the innumerable interruptions and distractions of a social life.

The artist must learn the difference between the *appearance* of an object and the *interpretation* of this object through his medium. Imitation is better done by photography, but to infuse reality with life and startle the observer into a new state of consciousness is to create something of one's own. There must be a spark before we can make a fire, and before art is born the artist must be ready to be consumed by the fire of his own creation.

Early training is of the utmost importance. The familiar slogan, "Catch them when they're young," is applicable to many human practices; it has special significance when applied to art students, religious training, and the taming of wild animals.

A great advantage is gained if the instincts of men and animals can be studied and directed by understanding the individual, rather than by traditional methods, which often restrain the natural impulses and cramp the imagination. For no two children are any more alike than any two animals. Even twins born within a few moments of each other and nursed under identical conditions develop widely divergent personalities.

In recent years a great deal has been done, in the educational field, to break down habits and theories of group teaching. The child is being considered as an individual, rather than as a mere number in a class. Great strides have been made in encouraging the child to do original work, which develops the imagination and forces the child to observe or invent mental pictures rather than to commit to memory other people's ideas. Their fancy and instinct to create respond to this system with alacrity and enthusiasm.

The training of a young pupil's mind towards a comprehensive understanding of art should include the exercise of concentration, the development of accuracy of observation, and the drawing from memory of visual impressions. The student should be stimulated to do just a little more and better work than is ever expected of him, to make his aim exceed his grasp, to surprise his teacher and himself a little by occasionally doing extra outside work. This constitutes a link of interest and understanding between the pupil and the teacher, a sort of after-hour companionship that can develop into a very useful influence. He should be made aware at an early stage of the actual brotherhood of man; an open-minded conception of racial types, with all their varying qualities and characteristics, should be instilled into his mind. So often students think that drawing continually from a nude white model is a sufficient experience. The whole world of animals, plants, nature, and all organic forms, as well as different races of man—everything in an ever-enlarging world holds a new challenge to the artist to understand its own particular character, anatomy, and psychology.

The artist should have tolerance, patience, and broad-mindedness, with an understanding of the eternal values and quality of thought rather than of words and acts, which so often belie the intention behind them. He should respond to the spiritual source of inspiration and reverence the eternal mysteries of life and death, constantly studying the correlation between the principles which form the basis of life and the arts.

The artist should prepare himself both consciously and subconsciously for an emergency need. He can never know what sudden demand may be made of him from any unexpected angle. He must be ready in his study to construct and interpret a human being, an animal, a tree, a fitting design for some architectural façade or lunette or fountain for a garden, a tombstone or a symbolic monument to commemorate a great deed of heroism.

The artist's interest should be stimulated in the study of great masters of the past, not only in their achievement but essentially to understand why these masters were great. Read the record of their lives, whereby it may be discovered that their qualities of greatness were based upon respect for truth, self-sacrifice to an ideal, and indefatigable courage and patience to carry out an inner vision, a secret hope to reveal a glimpse of eternity.

VI. Suggestions for a Practical Art Center

URING the past few years this country seems to have developed a real art consciousness, and in all directions one hears of new ventures being started to guide and instruct the public towards a more intelligent approach to art. With this growing trend in mind I venture to suggest the following plan for a practical art center for students and laymen. For those communities where funds are available the same methods for demonstrating the art and technique of painting and murals should be carried out, and above all there should be a department devoted to the science of light as affecting sculpture, moving pictures, and art in all its fields. In the following pages I shall deal with sculpture only.

There should be a collection of sculpture in many different mediums: marble, stone, alabaster, plaster, terra cotta, wood, bronze, aluminum, lead, coal, brick, cast stone, etc., and modern plastic materials; also drawings in pencil, charcoal, and pastels; water colors, oils, tempera, etc. These should serve to illustrate the suitability of certain materials to special subjects. The sculpture examples should show variety of treatment as well as of style: formal, personal, architectural, abstract, decorative; portraits, stylized and monumental, both in the round and in relief.

There should be cases of medals and coins, with the best examples from archaic and medieval times to the present day, and photographs showing how medals are reduced and struck, and explaining the galvano process and steel dies.

A collection of documents would include photograph albums of human types, and a few native art objects, carved weapons, etc., relating to the study of the races of mankind throughout the world. These native carvings of primitive peoples show their instinctive understanding of design and craftsmanship.

Exhibit cases would show stone- and wood-carving tools and the surfaces and textures that can be obtained by use of them; models, in sections, of sculpture in different stages of development: original clay sketch, plaster cast, gelatine negative lined with wax, the outer covering and core, raw bronze cast as it comes from the foundry, chased bronze cast, and the finished subject patined by acids.

Another case would show the sand-mold process, the sand pieces pressed around plaster model, the core and exterior molds, suspension pins, iron frames, or flasks, etc.

Another case would show how terra cottas are made, the clay pressed into its piece mold, final form and color after baking; the differences between Roman and other joints in plaster casting.

Sets of tools used in each stage of the process should be shown with the models, also acids and chemicals used to make patines; explanatory photographs of every stage of the work in the studio and in the foundry.

Shadow boxes would be equipped with indirect top, side, and foot lighting, controlled by separate switches to show the surprising effects of lighting sculpture from these different angles, both in the round and in relief.

A library of up-to-date good books on sculpture in all its phases would be especially important, as art students have not the time to hunt in libraries and museums and waste hours trying to extract some reliable and constructive information about technical problems of sculpture.

Labels in WHITE:	Would denote books on the history of sculpture in general.
BLUE:	Books on modeling and technique.
RED:	Stone and wood carving.
YELLOW:	Anatomy, dissection, and drawing.
GREEN:	Garden and architectural sculpture.
PURPLE:	Tools, equipment, stands, ladders, enlarging and reducing machines, etc.
GRAY:	Symbols, ornament, and lettering.
BROWN:	Medals and numismatics.
BLACK:	Chemistry, patining, and treatment of metals.
ORANGE:	Biographies and autobiographies of great sculptors.

A set of albums of photographs would show examples of ancient sculpture and the work of contemporary artists in alphabetical order, cross-indexed in chronological order.

There should be an information bureau where reliable advice could be given to art students. The National Sculpture Society's Red Book * should

* This is published and sold at 115 East 40th St., New York City.

be available. This lists the names and addresses of all the most reliable crafts-men, giving their special qualifications, materials for sale, tools and brushes, enlarging and reducing machines, studio equipment of all kinds, plaster casters, ornamental modelers, medal makers, foundries, potters, etc., includ-ing the best names in London and Paris.

Such a library and reference bureau should be directed and kept up to date by a well-informed and reliable manager. It would then be of the greatest value to any community.

There might be a series of lectures at the art center which would be in the form of discussions with the aid of practical execution and demonstration by experts following every stage of the process for a complete sculptural work. A temporary chairman would be chosen to direct each evening; he should be an expert in the subject of the lecture. After the lecture moving pictures could be shown, and a discussion between the students and laymen would be held for thirty minutes.

A practical sequence of subjects would be:

1. CLAY MODELING:	Advantages and disadvantages.
PLASTELINE:	" " "
ARMATURES:	For the support of clay and plasteline. Small sketches to show how the idea takes form in sculpture. (A sculptor would prepare an armature and build up a figure or a head and demonstrate how the basic construction is necessary before carrying on the work in detail.)
2. PLASTER CASTS:	Waste-mold process, gelatine process, plaster piece-mold process, Roman joints, keys, etc. Squeezing clay into piece mold.
3. ENLARGEMENT and REDUCTION:	Proportional dividers, pantograph. Explanation of Payne machine, Colas machine, and others. Making scale for compass enlargements; frames marked off with strings, squaring on paper for enlarging cartoons, and three-caliper system of posts for enlarging in stone, etc.
4. TERRA COTTA:	Preparation of molds and squeezing clay for terra cotta; baking, shrinkage, glazing and coloring.
5. METHODS OF COLORING:	Coloring plaster to look like bronze, stone, granite, etc.; waterproofing.
6. BRONZE CASTING:	(a) Sand process: advantages and disadvantages. Making the negative molds, core, and covering.

(b) Lost-wax process, gelatine and plaster piece molds. Preparation of wax (soft and hard); retouching of waxes; core supporters, gates and vents; mixture of light refractory materials for molding of waxes. Pouring of bronze at proper temperature; rough bronze finish and cleaning, either by acids or by sandblasting; chasing of bronzes and repairs; alloys; explanations of foundry equipment and implements.

7. BRONZE PATINING: An expert founder would direct this lecture. An assistant would work the blowtorch and apply the acids during the explanation. One of the students might assist in this lecture and gain practical experience thereby.

8. ELECTRIC WELDING: Nickel, aluminum, castings, electrolytic action of different metals.

9. ANCIENT HISTORY OF BRONZES: Alloys of Chinese, Egyptian, Roman, and Renaissance bronzes. Diseases or chemical alterations of bronzes exposed to the elements; reasons and preventions.

10. MARBLE, STONE, and WOOD CARVING: Equipment necessary for working on stone or carving wood. Use of pointing machine demonstrated. Surface textures obtained by various tools.

MOVING PICTURES: To be shown after the lectures. These would show different sculptors at work in their studios and the processes of casting and carving in stone, marble, or wood. A list of all available films along these lines should be kept up to date, and where they may be procured or rented and their cost; also names of reliable operators, projectors, etc. If fine still pictures exist, these could be made into slides and shown on the screen.

Of course, to make a complete unit of this suggested art center, there should be three well-equipped, spacious working studios: one for easel painting and mural painting; one for modeling and drawing; one for plaster casting and carving, and, if possible, additional space for a small foundry.

Each department should be under the direction of a gifted, competent artist, an expert in his own field and equipped with technical as well as imaginative powers.

The success or failure of such an enterprise would depend so largely on the personality and character of the artist directors that the greatest care should be given to their selection. The pupils should be permitted to watch their teachers at work in their own individual studios and gain thereby the impetus and lesson of the teachers' practical experience.

An interesting experiment has been tried out west, where the resident instructor in one university art school directs a "painting clinic." To this the students and local would-be artists bring their work to be set up before the class and diagnosed; their weaknesses are pointed out, and, if curable, the "doctor" director advises the best treatment.

This plan has met with enthusiastic response, and may build up many new and constructive ideas of teaching.

In every project of art education there should be evening and Saturday classes for those students who have to work by day to earn their living. These classes would be a great boon. Anyone who, after eight hours of work, still wants to continue his studies in the evening should be encouraged. If his day work is ornamental carving he would do well to spend his evenings drawing from life, or modeling in clay. The change of material would revitalize his interest, and many of his problems in carving could be studied and solved in clay. If he is engrossed in some problem of bas-relief composition, it would rest and stimulate him to work in the round or make drawings. If a stonecutter has ambition to improve his knowledge of form he could do no better than go to an evening course of lessons in clay modeling. The fact that the evening classes would bring together the most serious students and laymen should prove of mutual benefit.

I suggest that even architects might benefit from such lectures, gaining a clearer understanding of the actual problems that confront sculptors. Cooperation between these two lines of activity would not only bring about a less formal relationship, but it would undoubtedly result in better work.

The same applies to interior decoration. How often could a sculptor or painter suggest a suitable overmantel bas-relief panel, or some note of color in mosaic, or an original idea for a handrail designed in metal, which would give an unexpected interest to the decoration. I would even go so far as to say that if such a close partnership of the arts were established, we should find sculptors suggesting suitable places for mural painters to decorate, and the painters might think of just the right place for a gay little bronze in a room which needs waking up, or an original, well-designed standard lamp, or hanging fixtures for indirect lighting. Why should we limit ourselves so definitely? Will we not thus risk becoming "specialists" who know more and more about less and less? Is there anything wrong about making a useful object beautiful? Or could we feel again the thrill and pride of the olden-day craftsman who could make a lock and a key worthy of being shown in a jeweler's window?

To develop culture in a people, it is necessary to establish a standard of values; there must be an awakening and sensibility to beauty. There must be a discrimination between what is suitable for machine production and what must be kept in the handmade category. There is a vital difference between standards and standardization. There are certainly plenty of objects and materials which must be produced by machines, without forcing the handmade crafts to extinction. If those in control are broad-minded, and their judgment is based on sound principles of economic and aesthetic needs, the decision will be made without destruction to either the mechanic or the artistic craftsman.

The means must be found to recognize and distinguish the object of handmade excellence and protect this from the cheaper, less individual machine-made article which may serve the same purpose and sell for less money.

The scholarships for book learning are many, but those for craftsmanship are few. The powerful leaders of industry are just now beginning to realize how art can add quality and style to their production, and they are organizing special departments in their factories where the design and appearance of their engines, frigidaires, lamps, and furniture may be studied and improved under the expert eye of industrial, and not commercial, art designers. The commercial artist's province is more in line with advertising, fashions, and window dressing.

Intelligent use of the artist's mind should soon establish a standard of appearance which would create a general demand for better lines and shapes in all the products turned out in quantity by machines. Some of our largest motorcar and mechanical factories have already found it wise to engage a regular staff of artist designers. I found this to be the case in Detroit. There the painters' problem is to find the best color combinations for all the painting on the bodies of automobiles, while the modelers and craftsmen evolve new models, new streamlines, more compact and graceful shapes in which to house the various machines. If industrialists all over the country would awaken to this field of progressive action, the country would inevitably witness a renaissance of design and craftsmanship. The artist needs the demand for his efforts, and business and machines can in this manner help rather than destroy art.

It is providential that there are still many things that a machine cannot do in spite of lie detectors, robots, and long-distance radio controls. And these things live in the domain of the spirit; they are born of the mind and soul of those who are just a little removed from the sphere of commerce. Art remains forever apart from the grim calculations of business, machinery, and money.

The three dictators, time, quantity, and cost, have no dominion over the realm of art; but still, there must be a practical working solution found whereby not only machines but *art* will be made to function along the lines of public needs, and whereby both these factors in modern civilization will be considered essential and integral units of life and the necessity for their support recognized.

The body and the soul are indivisible and interdependent. Can anyone be conscious of the manifestations of nature in all its forms, its design in motion as well as in repose, and yet ignore the need of the universal and cosmic language of art? Can they still think that man is a separate, independent creature or mechanical genius who can exist by sheer accomplishment and profit, and disregard the age-old truth that all living atoms are but parts of the eternal whole, and that man, beasts, flowers, sun, moon, and the starry heavens are and forever will be bound together and held in the mighty hand of the Sculptor of the Universe?

PART TWO

PART TWO

VII. The Sculptor's Studio

TO build an ideal studio is the dream of many hopeful artists, but to accomplish this one generally goes through a series of errors and experiments. One generally ends up with the consoling conviction that in spite of unfavorable conditions of light, heat, or equipment it is still possible to do good work in a cellar or a garret, provided there is sufficient urge and ability to drive the artist over all physical obstacles. The creative impulse is often so compelling a force that the artist becomes merely a vehicle of expression for the idea, just as a mere pudding is the means of conveying a supreme sauce.

Once seized, the artist becomes deselfed to such a point that he will fight through darkness, cold, or hunger until his daemon releases him. His surroundings fade into oblivion and his world consists of the fierce struggle and the ultimate goal. The fact of achieving even a part of this goal makes one so happy that the proportions of the studio or garret shrink into insignificance.

However pleasant may be the feeling of triumph over one's surroundings, there still remains the fact that good light, practical working equipment, sharp tools, and an even floor can add greatly to the enjoyment of work and reduce the wear and tear of fatigue and nervous exhaustion.

"Everything in its place and a place for everything" is a good motto to follow in the sculptor's studio. There are so many tools and supplies constantly in use that the only way to avoid chaos and slovenly untidiness is to put things away after using them, and put them away *clean*. Hours are saved by this method, unless of course you can afford a staff of helpers and clean-up boys. It is far better for the student to learn how to keep order instinctively and not grow lazy and leave unpleasant jobs for others to perform. By doing things yourself you learn how to use your wits as well as your hands, and there will be plenty of occasions when helpers will not be available and when necessity will challenge you to invent the way out of a bad situation.

If space on the ground level is available, the heavy loads of sculptor's marble, stone, plaster, and clay can be more easily unloaded, handled, and stored if the flooring is reinforced and the trucks permitted to back directly through a wide entrance door. The stands on which marble is carved should be four-legged and heavy enough not only to carry weight, but to remain solid and steady while work is in progress. A turntable top, held by a strong wooden pin, enables the sculptor to turn the work at will (rub the inner surfaces of top and stand with hard soap for lubrication).

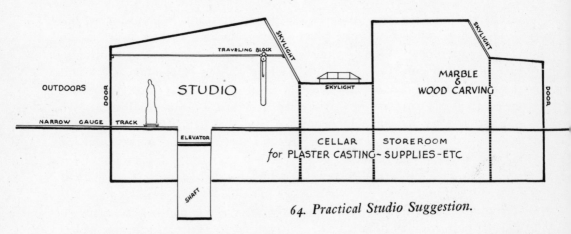

64. *Practical Studio Suggestion.*

When large models for outdoor work are being made, it is a great help to move these outside into a courtyard, or the open air if in the country, to judge them in sunlight and in shadow. A short section of narrow-gauge track, leading directly from the studio floor level, may be laid for this purpose, and makes the operation simple. Dollies or small low platforms on wheels are a great convenience; if in constant use over a wooden floor, the wheels may be of hard rubber to avoid marking the floor or dragging about noisy iron casters. The wheels should be set on ball bearings to enable them to turn easily in all directions. Where heavy work is often undertaken, another great asset is a traveling crane with block and fall (pulley and endless chain), which can move blocks of stone or heavy molds from one place to another with magic ease and safety.

Failing these luxuries, a few lengths of iron water pipes or even gas pipes come into use as rollers under heavy blocks. The "fifth wheel" is another indispensable part of studio equipment, when the stones are too large for working on a stand. Heavy timbers may be arranged, one pair crossed above the other, to the desired height and the fifth wheel set on top so that its circular ball-bearing track is well supported and the weight evenly distributed.

I once visited a studio where there was an extraordinary convenience for modeling large figures, in the form of an elevator which lowered or raised a square section of the flooring down into the cellar, so that the sculptor might work upon the head and shoulders of a heroic-sized figure without the need of ladders, and then raise up the figure above the studio floor level to the final height at which the figure was to be seen. This, of course, would necessitate quite a large cellar space below the ground floor of the studio entrance. This lower area could be used for making plaster casts, and it can be easily imagined what a convenience it would be when the figure is finished in the studio to be able to lower it out of sight and be spared all the difficulties, confusion, and debris of plaster casting.

65. Corner of My Studio in Paris. (PHOTO BY M. H.)

The section of the studio with a lower ceiling and small skylight, which extends beyond the main north skylight, is a very useful asset because the artist may back away from his work under this shadow-forming roof, and judge of the work in progress on which the north light falls at about an angle of 45°. It serves the same purpose as the hand of the familiar American wooden Indian figure, which always shows the Indian with his right hand shading his eyes so that he may see farther and better without having the glare of the light in his eyes.

Adjoining the studio there should be an extra room, with a cement floor that can be washed with a hose. In this room all the rough armature work, bending of irons, sawing of wood, and the keeping of the clay in bins should be attended to. If extra space is still available, another studio, continuing as in the line cut, could be used for marble and stone carving, as this operation spreads chips and marble dust to a considerable distance away from the work. It is not a good idea to have it done near a clay figure or near walls on which plaster casts are hung, as the chipping off of large pieces of stone will cause damage to the casts and clay.

Adequate space for storage of irons, wood, and other supplies should always be provided. It is convenient to set up a rack for the tools most often in use, directly over the workbench, so that they may be hung back in place and be within easy access when needed.

The element of light is of supreme importance. Besides the construction of a north-light skylight set in the roof of the building, it is essential to have a high side-light window as well, and where possible an overhead skylight as shown in the cut, so that work can be judged under all three conditions of lighting. When the light from the roof skylight is not needed, a lightproof shade can be installed underneath it and cut off all this light at will.

Water must be in a convenient place. A low, deep, iron sink under a threaded tap is useful, with a hose pipe attachment when needed. Gas also should be available for a blowtorch for patining bronzes. For night work, lighting by electricity is of course a serious problem, and there are endless modern appliances for its solution. A simple way is to string a long line of bulbs in a reflector along the north wall under the skylight. This will throw the light on your work at the same angle as the daylight enters. Extra wall outlets are needed for attaching special lamps. Indirect light is ideal if adequate, and splendid fixtures are available for this. Some artists prefer blue daylight bulbs, others yellow, and others the combination of both.

In Paris my studio was of the primitive type: coal stove; uneven, creaking

floor; leaking skylight, too flat on the roof; water only in the cellar (and
what a cellar!). Mushrooms and weird fungi seemed to sprout out of the
cracks in the walls, nourished by constant leaks and dampness. However,
I grew to love the companionship of the glowing, friendly stove, which
depended entirely on me for its fuel and winked its little red mica eye at
me when the draft was set to pull, and wintry dampness was driven away,
and the studio turned into a cozy shelter for work.

Most of the life-size figures for the Hall of Man in Chicago were built
up from the original one-third-size models (made on the journeys) in this
Paris studio, and the endless line of models and visitors from all the quarters
of the world made this little corner of the *impasse* a colorful and amusing

67. *Heavy Type Modeling
Stand for Carving Stone,
Turntable Top.*

66. *Mechanical Attachment
for Raising Turntable on
Modeling Stand.*

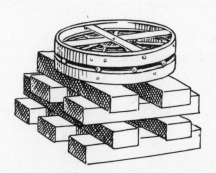

68. *Fifth Wheel Set on Heavy
Blocking.*

meeting ground for white, black, yellow, and red friends who frequently, after the late afternoon séances, would chat together over a glass of Dubonnet and exchange tales of Lombardy with those of Malay jungles or African deserts. Paris, the wonder city of all races, where poverty and bohemia know how to live together gracefully!

Almost anything may happen in a studio! An artist is liable to be called upon to do the most incredible things.

Studio emergencies range from first aid to the injured (cuts, bruises, and splinters are part of the day's work) and removing bits of marble from the eye of a fellow carver (and being quick about it), to mending a suddenly leaky pipe, bracing and reinforcing a platform or scaffolding which starts to give way in a vital spot, rigging up a block and fall or pulley and chain to a high beam, and training oneself to climb high ladders and work on narrow planks (for sooner or later one will be faced with the emergency of working on some dizzy height of a building to supervise the placing or finishing of some sculpture). If one has practiced a bit at home one's blood will freeze less quickly as one climbs a perpendicular ladder eighty feet high and walks out on a narrow plinth above the street and "sees the Fords go by."

It is not surprising to find studio helpers who are unable to stay up in the air at a height of fifteen to twenty feet and feel at ease. This often is a serious failing, for when the need occurs to draw up full-size cartoons for heroic figures, or the panels of a twenty-foot relief are to be modeled high up in the air, the men or women who do this work should have trained themselves beforehand so that they can feel safe to do their work without constant giddiness or fear. On the other hand, we often hold our breath with apprehensive admiration when we watch the acrobatics of expert craftsmen as they climb about scaffolding with absolute indifference and perfect equilibrium.

There is one unique studio man who stands high (six-feet-two) in his chosen profession. His name is Bill, and there is hardly a sculptor living in New York who does not know him or who has not heard of him in the annals of studio life. Bill is a Czechoslovak who has posed for almost every known statue of Lincoln, and who says of himself that he resembles Abe "from the feet down."

When a young lad, Bill had an ambition to become an artist. He studied drawing at the Pratt Institute, observed his fellow students, managed to sell a few illustrations to magazines, and developed a certain left-hand technique. His studies enabled him to understand art and be a wise critic. As he grew older he realized that his ideal was too far ahead of him and that the world was overcrowded with artists who couldn't quite make the grade. So he decided to give up trying to do original work and instead of this to study art through helping others to achieve their aims and take care of their studios, prepare their armatures and clay, and clean their tools. He lived for many years with Augustus Saint-Gaudens, and worked in his studio until the day of his death. Having chosen his line of action, he made it a profession, and he has won the admiration and gratitude of many sculptors.

His independent character accepts no halfway measures. When he takes on the job of cleaning a studio, the sculptor might as well move out and give Bill his keys. You can issue orders or suggestions as you like, but before long you will discover that Bill is doing the job his way and not yours, and the result is better than you had expected. He has found the way not only to be useful, but to make himself indispensable. Those of us who have been included in Bill's "key ring of sculptors" have felt the wonderful relief of mind as we turned the studio over to him when a long task was finished.

69. "Bill Working," by Malvina Hoffman, Jeu de Paume Museum, Paris.

It may resemble a sort of battlefield, with pieces of plaster, planks, and debris after the demolition of some large group that has been cast, wet rags, cigarette ashes, broken bits of wood, dirty brushes, and dust everywhere. This veritable chaos is tackled by Bill with a definite, methodical system. Everything is pushed into the center of the room, all refuse collected. Then all rags and tools are soaked in pails of clean water and Gold Dust. Next he tackles the edges of the floor, and cleans a space along the wall about four or five feet wide. "Elbow grease and half and half gas and oil, lady, that's the receipt." When these strips are thoroughly cleaned and rubbed to a polish, he starts in the center of the room again, scraping and wiping all the stands, stools, or ladders that have been in use.

These are then carried to the clean part of the studio and set against the wall. Then the soft broom is used again, forever pushing its way from the walls to the center of the room until finally only a narrow path is left unpolished. Sprawling on all fours, and waving his long powerful arms, he says, "Rub hell out of it, give till it hurts, Lady Hoff, you can't beat dirt any more than Snow White can fill Radio City unless somebody sweats for it, and takes pride in the sweating."

The last wringing out of cloths and they are hung over the sink to dry, pails all neatly stacked, and then a last cigarette and a tug at the old belt; Bill has transformed bedlam into a ballroom. Eying his work with satisfaction, he says, "All ready for another fancy dress party now, Lady Hoff. Do you remember that wild one we pulled here when Pavlowa cut her birthday cake up on those steam pipes and I danced with one of the wealthiest women of America? Gee, lady, that was a night! Remember the twenty-four little yeller chicks I had on my bonnet, and the blinking electric bulbs all over my white angel costume? And Gawd, could you ever forget René and Sam as the Fratellini brothers, in the Eighth Avenue union suits, dragging a dead flea in a hearse? Those were the days, Lady Hoff. And our neighbors the police all came to the party about dawn, and we had to push 'em out with a few late ones, so we could turn out the lights, and nobody knew the real policemen from the costumed ones! Well, so long, Lady Hoff, I'll be back in a few days. I've got to polish up Muriel Draper's flat and clean Herbert Adams's roof, and then I'll tackle your north skylight. All the young ones nowadays are afraid of balancing on top of a soapbox tied to the end of a fourteen-foot ladder, but it's pie to me, and I sure love to get the better of New York dirt. Here you are, lady, have a coffin tack on me." And offering me a cigarette he wheels about and disappears. And that's our Bill—God bless him!

70. *Assembling Sections of Bronze Casting, Showing Necessary Equipment of Ladders, Trestles, Etc., Enabling Several Men to Work at the Same Time Without Interference or Crowding, Rudier Foundry, Paris.*

71. Collection of Tools:

1. Proportional Calipers. 2. Triangle. 3. Carpenter Square. 4. Clamp for Holding Wood to Bench. 5. Basin for Mixing Plaster. 6. Flexible Brass Bowl for Plaster. 7. Half of Rubber Ball for Plaster. 8. Plaster Knife. 9. Spool of Solder. 10. Spool of Wire—Copper. 11. Clay Tool—Wire End. 12. Wire (Galvanized). 13. Double-ended Wire Clay Tool. 14. Larger Double-ended Metal Clay Tool. 15. Large Steel-headed Clay Tool. 16 to 24. Different Sizes of Modeling Tools. 25, 26. Plaster Tools, Flat Steel-notched Edge. 27. Claw Hammer. 28. Carpenter's Level. 29. Wooden Mallet. 30. Hardwood Clay Patter, Rough Surface. 31. Hardwood Clay Paddle, Smooth Surface. 32. Plaster Brush. 33, 34. Sharp Wire-headed Tools. 35. Plaster Finisher. 36, 37. Wire Wrapped on Steel—Tools. 38. Large Plaster Spatula. 39, 40, 41. Smaller Plaster Spatulas. 42. Plaster-finishing Tool, Saw-toothed. 43. Plaster Grater (Perforated Metal). 44. File. 45. Wire Brush for Cleaning Tools. 46. Hatchet. 47. Syringe for Spraying Water on Clay. 48, 49. Brushes for Shellac, Soaping, Etc. 50. Heavy Cutting Pliers. 51. Small Cutting Pliers. 52. Tin Shears. 53. Pliers, Medium-sized. 54. Pliers, Small. 55. Scissors. 56. Iron Tool to Bend Pipes and Irons (Square Shaft ⅞″): A = 1″ Slot; B = ½″ Slot; A to B 14″ Long. 57. Screw Driver. 58. Soldering Iron. 59. Plumb Line. 60. Drawing Compass. 61. Stone-pointing Compass. 62. Proportional Dividers. 63. Curved Caliper.

TOOLS

Archaeological records show us that the earliest stone tool makers were from southeastern Asia, and the tools found recently in the same locality as the "Pekin Man" in China are of about the same period of the Stone Age as those found in Java and Malaysia. Half a million years ago man fashioned his tools from river pebbles, and the "Java Man" may well have been the rival stonecutter of his northern contemporary craftsman.

It certainly amazed me to find how skilled are the primitive tribesmen in the South Pacific islands. With the crudest tools they carve most intricate patterns into the wooden prows of their canoes. The posts supporting the roofs of their forest dwellings are covered with bas-relief patterns, often intensified by bright colors. Every paddle, shield, and wooden implement is carved and decorated by native craftsmen so expert that they put many a high-brow sculptor to shame by their speed and skill.

The primitive learns to use his tools in self-defense, to make spears and bows and arrows, and the fact that his life depends on these makes him an expert. Now that this stark necessity of self-preservation has been removed from most of the civilized and educated people of the earth, the standard of hand training has sunk to a low level.

Most people know very little about their own hands. Their muscles are flabby and untrained, their fingers weak and unreliable. Watch an expert carpenter or stone carver working, and then try to repeat exactly what he has done, with the same material and identical tools. Impossible; the chisel slips, the stone either resists your blow entirely or looks like Swiss cheese with accidental holes punched into its surface. The very act of striking a chisel with a mallet becomes an exciting experience as the ability to do it develops.

As a simple test, just ask any would-be craftsman or sculptor's assistant to take two pieces of round pipe and fasten them together securely so they will not turn or shift. Give him a coil of wire and a pair of pliers (without wire cutters). Watch him closely and observe just how he goes about the work, how he handles the tool; whether he pulls steadily on the wire before and during the twisting, keeping both ends spread apart as they are twisted, or whether he just tugs and turns one end around the other, causing it to break off or slip open when a strain is put upon it. There is a right and a wrong way to do everything, and it is always a revelation to find fully grown people continually making the same mistakes, never having observed closely enough to copy the expert craftsman who has found the best method by long experience.

Fingers gradually respond to your wish, and tools become extensions of your fingers, responding more and more to the work demanded of them by the mind. The pupil should learn to temper and sharpen steel tools. The edge must be carefully watched and kept in perfect condition. Good workmen use good tools and take care of them with respect and often with real attachment. I have seen great sculptors stop their work and mend a broken tool with as much care as a jeweler would use in repairing a watch. One grows dependent upon certain tools. They seem to respond better than others, they cut clearly, they fit and balance in our grasp. They become reliable and trusted friends, and we should treat them as such, but we should not become slaves to them.

The clay tools that Rodin used were often homemade and rather crude, but they served his purpose and he knew their capacity and limitations and loved them. We in New York have great tool makers and shops that supply every article that any sculptor could need—slender wooden tools that have the beauty of line and balance of an Indian's paddle. Every variety of taste is catered to: there are delicate, tiny blades; strong, rugged, steel cutting tools; steel wrapped with wire to roughen a surface and pull the forms together. Then there are wonderfully delicate plaster-carving implements that curve their way between the edges and cut out deep places where clumsier ones could never reach. Plaster tools must be made of fine steel— strong and rigid and able to take rough handling and lots of pressure.

The plaster surface can be made to look like stone or marble or any desired medium by cleverly working over the forms with the right tools and with the knowledge of just how the desired results can be achieved. It is surprising (and something to beware of) how quickly the surface of a plaster can be completely ruined by the wrong use of tools or sandpaper.

A palpitating, living figure, modeled freely and well cast, can in a few moments be completely destroyed by an untrained hand smoothing out just the wrong places and scratching the surface with meaningless lines and accents.

The greatest danger (and this applies to marble surfaces as well) is the use of small rasps and sandpaper in the effort to make the work appear more finished, when in reality what generally happens is that the life and vigor of the original clay has been smoothed to a lifeless state.

NECESSARY EQUIPMENT

Human skeleton—articulated and hung on a supporting iron.

Two good anatomical plaster figures: one in repose, one in action.

A model stand about 18″ high with revolving top, 4′ x 4′.

Proportional calipers.

Good set of modeling tools (6 or 8).

Workbench with strong vise.

Rolls of lead pipe (½″ and 1″ diameter).

Rolls of galvanized wire—heavy and light gauge.

Pair of strong pliers (with wire cutter).

Pair of metal-cutting shears.

Half dozen brushes from ½″ to 2″, flat and round.

Screw driver, reinforced handle.

Two hand saws (1 cross cut).

Claw hammer.

Metal hack saw, removable blades.

Plumb line. Square. Level.

Assortment of screws.

Assortment of nails: 2″ wire, 1¼″ zinc flat heads galvanized, and 3″ finishing nails.

Can of orange shellac. Can of wood alcohol.

Square ¼″ and ½″ irons for armatures.

Set of 3 wide steps with 2′ x 2′ top.

Ladder 5′ high. Ladder 10′ high.

Bundle of laths for armatures, also several ⅞″ thick pine boards 4″ and 6″ wide.

Grindstone.

Sharpening stone.

Strong penknife.

One 6′ folding rule.

Two or three good modeling stands—three legs, mechanical means of raising and lowering the height of the top.

A carpenter's tool chest, with plane, brace and bits, chisels, etc.

Adjustable-top drawing table.

T square. Yardstick.

VIII. *Anatomy, the Human Machine*

*That true bible as we count it of the hu-
man body and of the nature of man . . .*
(VESALIUS, 1561)

THE wonders of the human machine, with its multiple activities and
elaborate system of co-ordinated units, can sometimes be most easily
explained by comparison with certain mechanical engines. For today,
almost everyone knows something about machinery. Is this not the machine
age?

Before jumping on a motorcycle or buying a car, it is generally considered only reasonable to understand its works and what methods must be
used to mend it if there is a breakdown of either electrical or motive force.
It always amazes me that people can leave all such details to either a chauf-
feur or a mechanic, and yet enjoy riding thousands of miles with no interest
whatever in how they are being propelled through space. They would be
thrilled at the marvels which go on under the hood of their car and under
the floor of the car's body—internal-combustion engines, exhaust valves,
carburetors, gearboxes, the complexities of oiling and lighting systems. Even
though they may seem too difficult and fatiguing to understand, yet the
realization of the perfection with which they perform their duties, responding to the touch of the driver's hand or foot, would seem to me rather to
add a thrill to the enjoyment of a fine car.

It is in mechanical terms that one can sometimes explain many of the
baffling conditions of a human being's mind. How often can we say, "So
and so certainly needs to have his brake linings renewed!" Or if someone
loses his sense of direction and wobbles in his mental decisions, his state is
clearly recognizable when described as, "So and so needs his steering wheel
tightened up, there's too much play in it. Look at the tracks his wheels
make on the road!"

The principles of many mechanical inventions were no doubt derived
from the observation of human muscles and bones. The multiple system of

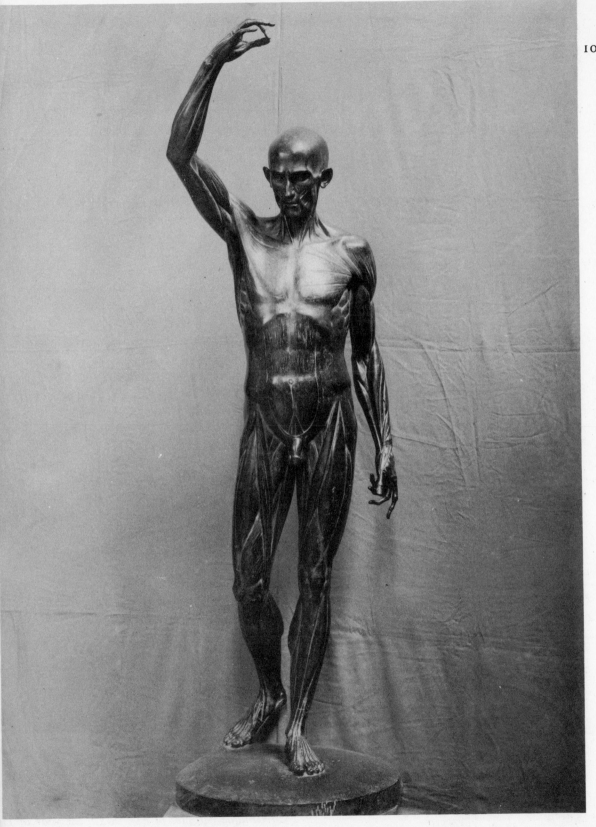

72. *Anatomy Figure by Jean Antoine Houdon.* (GIRAUDON)

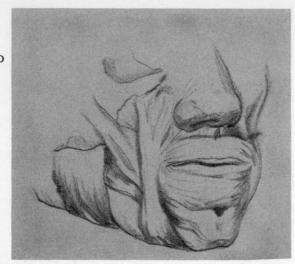

73, 74. *Head and Facial Muscles, Drawn by M. H.*

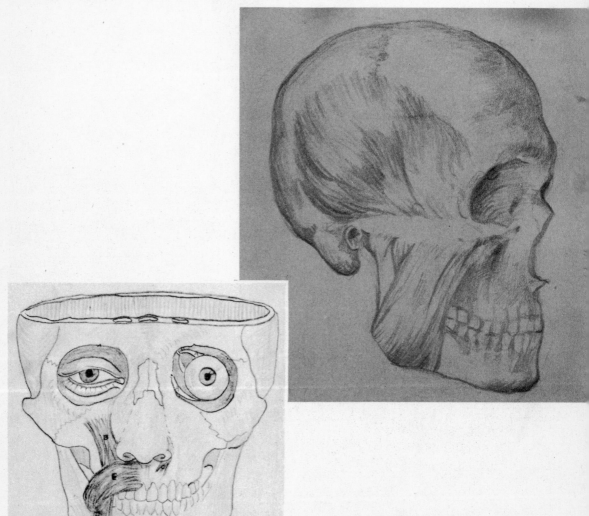

75. *Section of Skull, from Quain, 1836. a. Show Two Oblique Muscles of Eyeball. b. Elevator of U per Lip. c. Depressor Muscle of Wing of Nose. d. E vator of Lower Lip. e. Orbicular of Lip.*

nerve messages, distribution of energy, lubrication, leverage, and heat generation probably revealed to mechanical minds many of the modern marvels of the machine age.

Leonardo da Vinci has left us evidence of his profound study in a wonderful set of anatomical drawings. These are kept in the library at Windsor Castle. In 1925, when I was studying in this library, I marveled at the many discoveries that da Vinci made in relating the human machine to the world of mechanics.

In 1919 Sir Arthur Keith gave a series of lectures in London called "Engines of the Human Body." These lectures were composed for an audience of young listeners, and the explanations were made so graphic and simple in mechanical terms that everyone could clearly understand all the

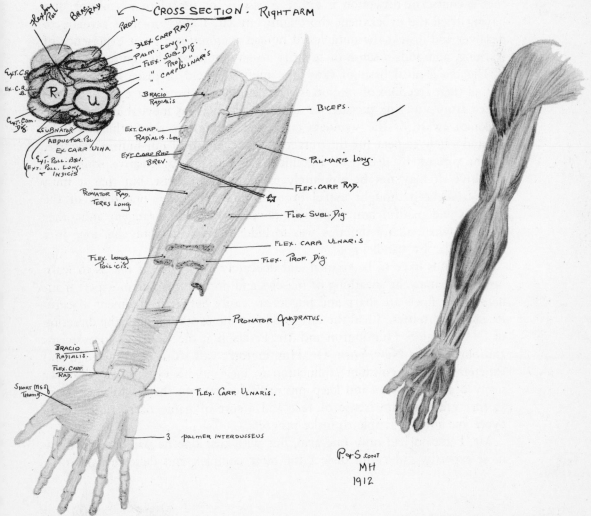

76. *Right Arm, Muscles Cut and Section View to Show Relation of Bones to Muscles, by M. H. at the College of Physicians and Surgeons, 1912.*

77. *Right Arm, Dissected and Drawn by M. H. at the College of Physicians and Surgeons, 1912.*

circulatory, muscular, and glandular problems of the human body. It was my privilege to make a portrait of Sir Arthur Keith in London in 1929. A great deal of his brilliant knowledge was revealed to me during the sittings, and during the years in which I modeled the racial types for the Field Museum, Sir Arthur's keen eye was constantly watching over the progress of the work and calling my attention to many observations which I should otherwise never have made.

The understanding of anatomy and bone construction should be part of the mental equipment of every sculptor. It should be studied and memorized, and stored away in the subconscious mind where it may be referred to at any time.

There are those who will smile and raise their eyebrows if it is suggested that a course in dissection is either necessary or useful to a sculptor; but having tried the experiment thoroughly myself, I must say that actually to discover and dissect the miracles of human anatomy is a great experience of learning, and adds a sense of security to any study of the figure.

The mechanical basis of how the joints are held in place and yet permitted their freedom of motion is a revelation which cannot ever be appreciated from studying pictures or anatomy charts. It is inevitable that if one becomes aware of the wonders concealed under our skins, there will be created a new respect for the miraculous mechanism of our human machine.

The process of dissection is difficult, and to many sensitive souls it is repulsive. It may not be absolutely essential to an artist, but that it must once have been thought useful becomes apparent when one reads of the arduous and painful hours spent in dissection by Michelangelo and other masters, when such a practice was forbidden and could only be done in a secret cellar by candlelight.

The hands have to be trained and delicately controlled if one is to learn how to separate the sheathing of muscles and do the work in an expert manner. The scalpels are sharp and fingers are easily cut if any moment of carelessness is permitted. I had the rare good fortune to study under the direction of Dr. George S. Huntington and Mr. Peterson at the College of Physicians and Surgeons in New York. Dr. Huntington's vast store of knowledge and experience was a constant stimulation to me, and his eyes would discover many beautiful things and keep my mind focused on them while working, so that gradually my sense of fear and a sort of panic of repulsion were overcome and I was able to make progress.

Mr. Peterson had only one arm, but with that one he painted and drew most expertly and could dissect the most complex and delicate parts of a

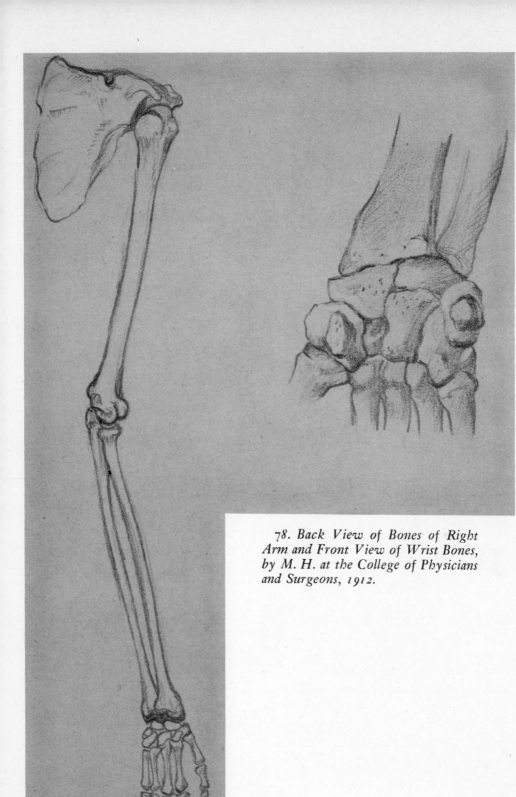

78. *Back View of Bones of Right
Arm and Front View of Wrist Bones,
by M. H. at the College of Physicians
and Surgeons, 1912.*

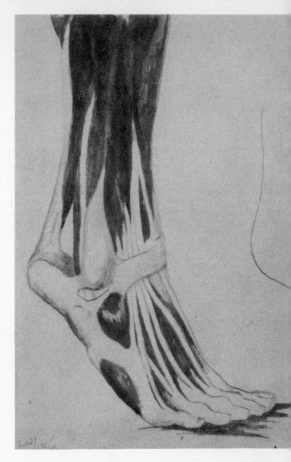

79, 80. Right Leg and Foot, Dissected and Drawn by M. H. as Preliminary Study for a Dancing Figure, College of Physicians and Surgeons, 1912.

figure with a skill that has seldom been equaled. His pupils would feel ashamed at their own clumsy performance, especially when he would watch us and then take our scalpel and show us how easily he could divide the arteries and veins and sheathing of muscles, never tearing or cutting the delicate tissue of his material.

It is impossible in a short chapter on such a subject as anatomy to give more than a few suggestions that may interest the student in carrying his studies further, but it is certain that if the would-be sculptor does not realize the importance of a thorough grounding in anatomical construction, he will never be able to interpret the human figure with security, nor will his work ever have that *indescribable authority that asserts itself in a real work of art.*

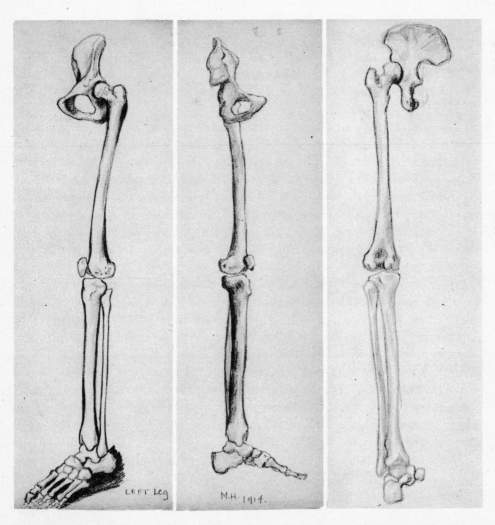

81, 82, 83. Leg Bones, Front, Side, and Back, by M. H., College of Physicians and Surgeons.

IX. Drawing and Modeling

DRAWING

You can become drunk in any art on your own emotion—arriving at no results at all. While working of course you must suffer, you have absolutely no pleasure, only the effort and pain. One way is to play, the other is to WORK.   (PADEREWSKI)

THE most important foundation for the making of a good sculptor is the ability to draw well. This cannot be overemphasized. It is a *sine quà non*.

The student should always carry a sketchbook in his pocket and note down the visual impressions of what goes on about him at all hours. Whether he drives in a car or rides in a subway or bus, he can always learn something from an accidental expression of the passenger opposite, or the folds of cloth in a dress, or the way light falls sharply across the features of a fellow traveler. He must constantly observe and memorize what passes before him in the endless panorama of life. In a real emergency one can usefully pose before a mirror to study oneself. Fatiguing as this may often be, it will help to teach you drawing.

To draw your own left hand in every position, or your own feet, will give you a good problem in foreshortening. Simple objects on the table, or the interior of the studio with all its strange contents of equipment, will serve a purpose to the student who knows how to develop his own technical ability.

Experiment with hard and soft pencils and charcoal, and find out what a vast variety of line and shading is possible. Try Conté crayons, hard and soft, and square chalks. Break the sticks, and use them for wide strokes—practice every kind of pressure for intensifying values, and control the sharp edge for defining outlines.

Study the old masters and try to understand their methods of handling ink

84. Drawings by Raphael, The Louvre. (GIRAUDON)

*85. Drawing of Hand Holding
Violin Bow, Attributed to Leonardo da Vinci, Ambrosiana Library, Milan.*

*86. Drawing by Michelangelo,
Buonarroti Gallery, Florence.*
(BROGI)

wash, pencils, and etched designs. It is interesting to learn the process of lithography, drawing your design with wax crayons on the velvety prepared surface of the lithograph stone. This practice is excellent training. You are forced to be sure of your strokes, as corrections on the stone are really taboo. In the inking and pulling of proofs by a hand press, the artist discovers endless new effects and scope for his imagination.

87. Crayon Drawing by Ivan Meštrović.

88. "Father Limet," by Malvina Hoffman, Charcoal and Chalk, Paris, 1922.

89. "*Breton Woman*," *Charcoal Drawing
by Jean Julien Lemordant.*

90. "*Cambodian Dancer*,"
Wash Drawing by Rodin.

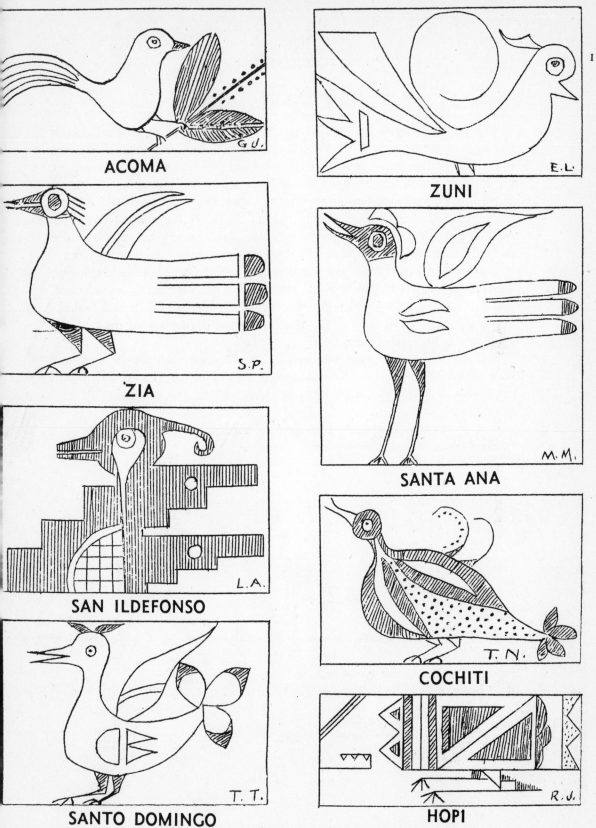

121

ACOMA

ZUNI

ZIA

SANTA ANA

SAN ILDEFONSO

COCHITI

SANTO DOMINGO

HOPI

91. Drawings of Birds by American Indian Children.

CLAY SKETCHES

The sculptor begins his task of interpretation by making a small sketch either on paper or directly in a small clay model. This first expression must suggest in its form and design all the essential proportions and meaning of his finished work. If the work is destined for some formal architectural façade, or for some garden, or an interior niche, the sculptor should make a scale model of the proposed setting so that his figure may be studied in its relative proportion to the surroundings. He should carry his sketch to the more finished state of a small scale study. By developing his idea in this way, he may feel free to try various combinations and designs, always keeping in mind their relation to the ultimate setting; and by this process of selection and careful study from all angles, he may avoid many pitfalls and feel security in going ahead with the large-sized figure, having solved most of the problems in his small model.

It is well to make a great number of clay sketches to obtain the technical skill of handling clay—in this manner learning how to express an idea in small size, with no essentials left out, but without the confusion of any superfluous details.

It is an inevitable source of interest to see the original clay study of a finished piece of sculpture with which one is familiar.

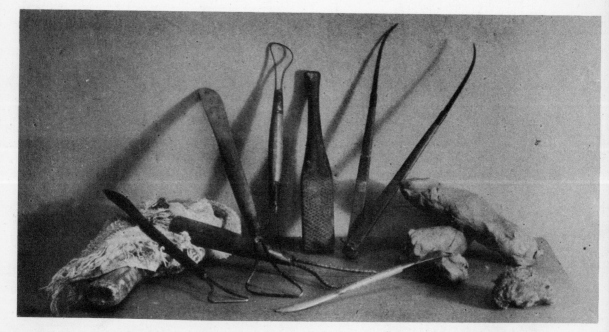

92. Six Clay-modeling Tools and Measuring Compass. (BERNES MAROUTEAU)

93, 94, 95. Development of an Idea, "The Eternal Idol," by Rodin.

Plaster Sketch.

Marble, Rodin Museum, Paris.

Bronze, Rodin Museum, Paris.

124

Original Sketch.

Plaster Scale Model of the Complete Monument.

Final Bronze Version of the Equestrian Statue Before Setting on Pedestal.

˙MODELING

*By facing this ugly world, by ranging wide
enough in it afar and above and below—
in Nature or in one's fellows or in oneself
one can find beauty—one can even create
beauty.*   (HAVELOCK ELLIS)

When modeling a head, it is well to start work some distance away from
the north skylight; then shift the position of the sitter and your work nearer
to the skylight. In this way you can change the angle of the light. A new
set of planes will suddenly show themselves, because the light, instead of
falling on the front surface of the subject and work, will come from almost
directly above. The subject should sit so that his head, your work, and your
eyes are on about the same level.

Before considering the head finished, place the living model and the
clay against a side light, so that they become sharp silhouettes; then, by
slowly turning them around, you will be able to judge the accuracy of the
drawing of every outline, for the form in the round is made up of an
endless series of planes and outlines, seen from every angle. This includes
the drawing from above and below, as well as from the front, side, three-
quarter, and back views.

It is frequently noticed in the work of beginners that the modeling of the
head lacks solidity; something uncertain in the construction is generally the
cause of this.

By looking up at the head from under the chin we can quickly notice
where the construction has been neglected or badly built up. One cheek-
bone may be found to be set farther forward in the face than the other, or
one eye is too deeply set under the brow. This will give the face a curious
weakness in its general effect.

This fault will not be so evident if the work is lighted from a window,
but if it is lighted from directly above, or if light is held under the chin,
it will immediately accentuate the defect and help the sculptor to judge of
his errors.

Have a steady modeling stand with a revolving top. Keep a wet sponge
on the stand to keep your hands clean. Avoid clay crumbs. Don't drop
clay all over the floor, and do not smear it all over the stand and yourself
and a lot of tools. Use it only for *modeling*. A good workman never makes

a mess, and if he does he cleans it up promptly without waiting to be told to do it by others.

When you stop working, wash your tools and dry them. Do not carelessly leave them in a pail to soak. They will soon crack and decay if you do. This applies to other people's tools as well as your own.

Wrap your clay figure carefully in clean, wet cloths. If the cloths are soaked in a pail of water, wring them out before applying them to the clay. Otherwise the excessive moisture will dissolve and injure the surface modeling.

If the figure is in action, or has delicate detail, take a few wooden sticks or bend a strong wire (galvanized) and push the ends into the clay so the cloths will be held away from the surface. It is sometimes advisable to construct a light wooden frame and cover the top and four sides with oilcloth, woolly side inside. This covering can be sprayed with water and, when thoroughly soaked, placed over the clay figure instead of cloths.

Shellac the wood of the frame to prevent the wood from warping, etc. It is well to lay a rolled damp cloth all around the base to keep out air and prevent quick drying. When fastening the armature pipe to a wooden base, be sure this base is large enough to support such a cage and the wet cloth outside of its frame; or else make it small enough to go completely inside the frame, which can rest on the top of the modeling stand just as well and better, for the larger the cage the less likely one is to knock off projecting hands or drapery when lifting it on and off. When the cage is heavy and unwieldy, hang it by wires to a cord which can be run over a pulley on the ceiling at one end of the studio, lifting the cage by the rope directly above the stand, and guiding the lower edge with the other hand. The cage may be left suspended and out of the way until needed. Then, at the end of the day's work, wheel the stand directly under the pulley and lower the cage carefully (avoid knocking off a few fingers in the bargain). If you intend to leave the clay for some time, spray it lightly and leave a wet sponge inside the cage as well.

Heavy cages can also be made to open on one side, so that the work can be examined and sprayed without lifting. If you have a removable side, be sure that it fits snugly and is held tight all around when closed by hooks and staples.

The first clay which is applied to the armature should be firm and solid in its consistency. If too soft it will not hold its shape or serve as a reliable foundation upon which to build up the rest of the work. Avoid mud pies, and remember that when your clay is right it will not smear all over your hands, but will have a plastic consistency. You must learn to use it neatly, for otherwise you will always remain an amateur.

To learn to manipulate clay and make it obedient is a vital step. It has a way of drying or crumbling in a manner disconcerting to the beginner. A student should learn from the start to apply the clay with definite purpose and form, not merely squeezing lumps along the armature in meaningless shapes. The feeling of the form and pose should be in every piece of clay as it is firmly set up in place.

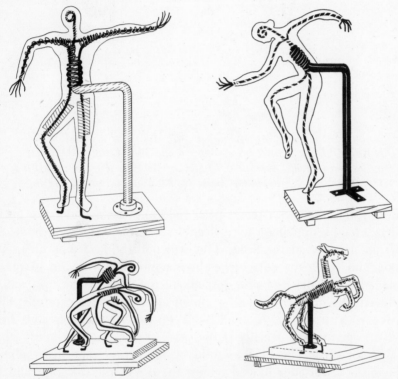

99. Four Types of Armature: Single Figures, Horse, and Group of Two Figures, Drawn by M. H.

A practical armature for a head is one-inch-diameter iron pipe, one foot long, threaded into a flange which is firmly screwed into a seven-eighths-inch wood base having two strong cleats underneath to prevent warping and to facilitate lifting in case of need. Into this hollow pipe insert a hollow lead pipe just a size smaller, about twenty-six inches long. Turn the upper end over in a ring and fasten to this two or three good "butterflies"—small flat pieces of wood three-quarters of an inch wide and two and a half inches long, held in a cross by copper or galvanized iron wire and suspended at different angles from the lead circle. Keep in mind the mass and silhouette of the head to be built up on these supports, so that you always allow for enough clay between the pipes, wood, etc., and your finished surface.

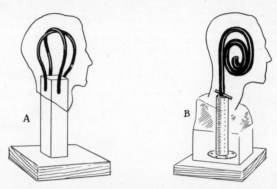

100. Two Types of Armature for Modeling a Head: a. Clay Is Built Too Low on This Armature and Pose Cannot Be Shifted. b. Type of Head Armature That Can Be Raised from Iron Pipe Held by Pin, and Permits Changing Pose or Height of Head.

If during the work you feel a need for more space under the neck and shoulders, etc., by drawing a wire cleanly around and through the neck you can lift up the mass of the head. This will pull the lead pipe up inside the iron one, and when the correct height is established you can drive a long wire nail through the lead pipe just above the edge of the iron one. This will prevent the head from sinking down after you have carefully filled in the space with firm clay. A small block of wood sometimes adds firmness to such an operation, especially if the angle of the head is slightly changed or tipped forward. The block should be in front rather than behind the lead pipe, the lower edge braced against the rim of the iron pipe and firmly attached by wire.

If it is intended to model shoulders on the portrait, a strong crosspiece of wood should be hung by wires wrapped around the lead pipe so they cannot slip down over the iron one when weight is added. Clay is cheap; you can afford to use it freely, and too much armature is often a nuisance.

Of course every sculptor works out his own ideas in building up armatures; some prefer an entire wooden construction, or the double lead pipe ovals fastened to the sides of a wooden upright post.

I have found the iron pipe and flange most practical, especially when I have been working while traveling in far countries. The pipes can be un-screwed and packed away easily. Wood often decays and breaks under the wet clay load.

There are very complicated and impressive-looking armatures made and for sale, but the homemade article, if constructed by a good craftsman, gen-erally answers his need better and gives him useful practice in handling his tools and relying on his own intelligence.

THE HEAD

He only moves toward the perfection of his art whose criticism surpasses his achieve-ment. (LEONARDO DA VINCI)

Before a student starts out to model a head it would be well for him to study a human skull. This he should copy in clay as exactly as possible. Then without looking at the skull or his own copy, he should do it over again from memory. If at first you don't succeed—try, try again. When the student has gone as far as he can, he should check up on the original skull and correct his errors.

After this he should make a careful drawing of all the facial muscles from an anatomy chart and a plaster anatomical cast. Again he should repeat this entire operation from memory. Slavish copying does not achieve the same result as intelligent memorizing.

When thoroughly familiar with the facial and neck muscles, he should use plasteline and lay these muscles on the surface of the skull on one side only. This will give him a vivid demonstration of how much goes on be-tween the bony surface and the outer skin of the face. It will also show him what muscles are used to chew and move the jaw; why nostrils flutter and are not rigid; how eyes open and shut; what smiles are made by, and what causes wrinkles and hollows in some places and soft flabby folds in others.

He should then study the construction of the neck and shoulder muscles; this will enable him from the start to avoid the beginner's mistakes which are usually caused by ignorance of just these facts and laziness or inaccuracy in observation. There is a wonderful group of muscles that spring from the shoulders and back to support the head firmly, yet still allow great flexibility. They swing up from the body like the roots of a tree growing from the earth, drawing their strength from many directions, and forming a protective

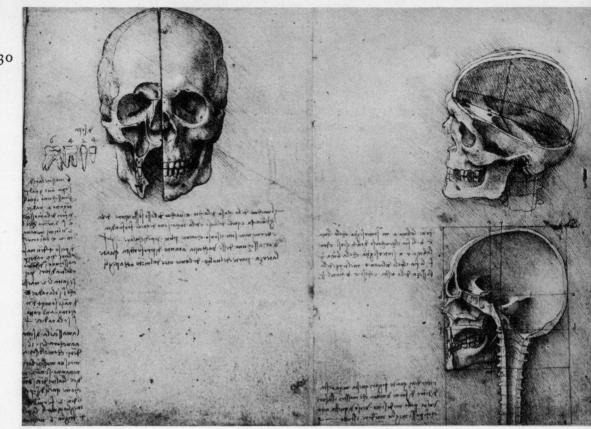

101. Drawings of the Skull by Leonardo da Vinci.

covering for the vital nerves and throat passages within the column of the neck.

It may be well for the student to model a life-sized—or better still, twice-life-sized—study of each feature, ear, eye, nose, and mouth. By making the size larger, it will be easier to build up all the details which form the individual features. It must be remembered, however, that all the races of man have their own particular problems in the widely varied character of their facial bones and muscles.

It is good practice, when you feel that you are safely familiar with all the varieties of the white race, to make a few careful studies of the Chinese, Indian, and Negro types. You will discover a new world of problems, each one challenging you in a new direction.

These racial distinctions are not limited to the head only, but apply to all the parts of the body—shoulders, torso, legs, arms, hands, and feet, and typical gestures and characteristic poses.

In studying the racial types during my trip around the world for the Field Museum of Chicago, I was constantly amazed at the never-ending variety of form and expression that I encountered.

PORTRAITS

I will not be afflicted at men's not knowing me;
I will be afflicted that I do not know men.
(CONFUCIUS)

In 1907, while struggling with the problems of painting and studying under John Alexander at Miss Veltin's school, I made two attempts to paint my father's portrait. He was very patient with me and posed a great many hours while playing the piano. I did one portrait in pastel that turned out quite satisfactorily—but when I had finished a second one in oils, I was so dissatisfied that I decided I must try to make his portrait in sculpture.

The third and even the fourth dimensions of art had begun to possess me, and I could not escape their drag. Never having seen a sculptor build up a life-sized head, I managed to work out a strange contraption consisting of an empty tomato can inverted over the end of a piece of kindling wood which I nailed onto a box, and by wiring bits of wood around the can I was able to keep the clay from slipping down—or so I innocently thought.

With this covered, I began father's portrait. He would pose while practicing, and neither of us spoke; he watched me, and knew I was at grips with something far bigger than either of us. He was seventy-eight years old and knew the battles that were ahead of me and behind him. I felt all this profoundly, as if my destiny were at stake. Could I make myself an instrument to this driving, unknown force, or could I not? I was consumed with a passionate consciousness that if I could do a good portrait of father, something of his art and integrity might be caught in my own art, and would never leave me.

Then suddenly and without warning, one night the inadequate armature gave way, and when I uncovered the head the next morning the neck had broken and half the clay had slipped down. I was dismayed and unhappy, not knowing what I should do, when the door opened and a friend came in accompanied by a stranger who turned out to be Gutzon Borglum, the sculptor. His engaging smile turned to surprise when he caught sight of the distorted mass of clay on the table! When I told him of my dilemma, he wasted no time on words. "Come along with me to my studio at once, and I'll show you how to build an armature. This portrait of your father is a good start, you can build another from this one without bothering your father to pose, and then go ahead in safety, no more amateurish beginnings." He took me by the arm and walked me around the corner to his studio. I was so delighted that I could hardly speak.

On entering the vast, high-roofed studio, the light fell in a white shaft from a great skylight above. I had never seen or even dreamed of such a space to work in; my heart pounded and I could only wave my arms about, exclaiming, "But one's soul could fly in such a place! Will you let me work here a few days?"

Mr. Borglum showed me the box of iron and lead pipes, a tool chest, and the clay bins. Rolling up his sleeves, he selected the necessary pieces and quickly demonstrated with his strong, sure hands how an armature should be constructed and the clay manipulated to an even consistency and pressed firmly around the pipes and wooden "butterflies." I remember every moment that was spent in the exciting atmosphere of that studio. I went out exhilarated, with a sense of exaltation for which I shall always be grateful.

Mr. Borglum and I had many talks about Rodin, whose work he admired ardently; this added to my enthusiasm for European study.

Having made a marble portrait of my father in New York, and one in bronze of Samuel Grimson, I knew when I sailed for Europe in 1910 that my mind was becoming more and more focused on sculpture, and that portraiture was a special and important factor in my program of study.

New worlds of beauty were revealed to me, and I met many types of men and women; I found myself amazed and bewildered at the fathomless range of human character. I would prowl about the streets studying and sketching the faces of artists, workmen, and ragpickers, the happy children sailing their boats in the Luxembourg pond, the concierges, the gendarmes, and the never-to-be-forgotten types of prewar cocher, or cab driver.

By fortuitous circumstance my mother and I were often invited to meet the most interesting creative artists of Paris, and to my curious and hungry mind all these contacts gave a vital stimulation. My imagination was constantly fed by surprises and discoveries, delights and disillusions, and my determination to learn French thoroughly was fired by the desire to understand and be able to interpret this new world of literature, art, and especially humanity.

I cannot stress too strongly the necessity and advantage to any art student of learning the language of France, and by this means being free to explore the wonderland of her literature and her art, and learn directly, rather than by translation or interpreters, what it is that constitutes her charm and her aesthetic supremacy.

To be able to interpret one's fellow man, one must love and understand humanity. Try as we may to fathom the character of another human being, we are always aware of something beyond what we can see or feel. A good way to learn about others is to examine yourself mercilessly and realize that most people are going to hide behind some sort of exterior personality until they feel that you are not hiding and that you are ready to play the game without masks or falseness of any kind.

There must be a common sympathy or understanding established between the sitter and the artist, for it is not, as is often believed, only three dimensions that are demanded of a portrait, but four, and this fourth one is the psychological atmosphere of the personality which must add expression and character and the endless variations of mood. The double-sidedness of most faces should be noted, also the difference of the profile as seen from the right or the left side and the interpretation of the hieroglyphics that record an inner emotional life. The face must be studied from above, below, three-quarters; every fractional motion makes a new profile for the artist to observe against the light, and reproduce, if not exactly, at least with as much accuracy as is necessary to reveal the character he is trying to portray.

A psychological analysis of the subject should be made by the artist, but deductions of this kind must be based on years of observation. Study all manner of men and women, as well as the animal kingdom, for animals often teach us lessons about humans, whether we like to believe it or not.

Sometimes the subject is shy or self-conscious when sitting upon a model's stand, and it is wise in this case to let him rest often and then watch closely what he looks like when walking about, or smoking, or in a completely relaxed and unself-conscious mood. These rest periods are often more revealing than the actual posing.

The basic characteristics and features of a race must be studied, for there are individual types that represent a race, and types that represent a country or a special locality, and types that fit nowhere—"extras." Some people are so full of inhibitions that their faces become like masks; they adopt some safe expression and hide behind it for years. There are inherited forms of family characteristics, self-made lines, and then there is the businessman's "poker face"; all these are problems for the portrait sculptor to fathom.

Muscles are developed differently in every face. There are eyes that smile and crow's-feet that record these smiles; eyes that are sad and lids that droop and give a weary look to them. Our two eyes can look at only one point at a time, so we retain a composite memory picture of a face, it being difficult to isolate one side completely from the other. There is generally one expression which is more habitual than another and by which we are recognized. We must learn to indicate the color of eyes, and their expression.

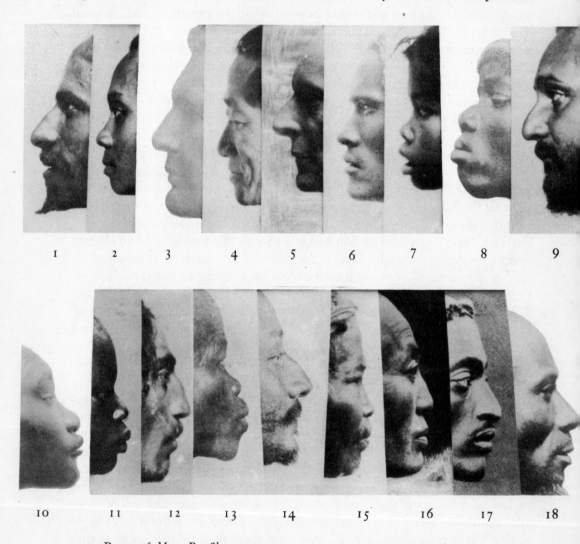

102. *Races of Man, Profiles:*

1. *Berber—Africa.* 2. *Dyak—Borneo.* 3. *Nordic—North America.* 4. *Chinese.* 5. *French.* 6. *Somali—Africa.* 7. *Jakun—Malay Jungle.* 8. *Zulu—Africa.* 9. *Kabuli—Northwest India.* 10. *Mangbetu—Africa.* 11. *Batwa—Africa.* 12. *Arab.* 13. *Bushman—South Africa.* 14. *Singhalese—Ceylon.* 15. *Jakun—Malay Jungle.* 16. *Mongolian—Asia.* 17. *Hamite—Nile, Africa.* 18. *Dahoman—Africa.*

Lips and the meaning of mouth shapes—there are endless ways to suggest the design of color on lips, as distinct from their form; watch for the subtle little edge of light that plays along the ridge of the lips.

Analyze ears; study the meaning of ear shapes, the way they are attached to the head, their subtle differences as seen from a three-quarter view or from below. Look for the signs of health or illness indicated in facial forms and scars of suffering or renunciation; all these things are written in the indelible lines of time and experience.

Smiles—how mad, how sad, how glad they can be! And what wells of silent suffering they sometimes try to camouflage!

The nose and nostrils constitute a whole chapter of study. The little planes that catch high lights, the way the bridge is set under the brow—how infinite is the variety of noses, when one observes the white, yellow, and black races in this particular feature alone! The shape of each nose as seen from below gives an unmistakable expression to the face, and the way the upper lip fits into the little valley which surrounds the nostrils is a subtle detail which should not be overlooked.

The idea that a likeness is the main object of a portrait is misleading, for a sculptor should be far more concerned in the making of a work of art than in merely reproducing the features of his subject in a speaking likeness. Sound movies do just this, and far better. Also there are never two people who agree as to what anyone really does look like. One remembers him smiling, another always sees him in a serious mood. One is sure the eyes are too small, and a fourth is perfectly certain that his lips curled back more and his nostrils were wider.

Try as we may, we are beaten before we start if we attempt to make just a likeness. An enlarged photograph fills that need and takes far less time, trouble, space, and money. I have heard a portrait well defined as "a likeness of a person, with something wrong about the mouth!"

There are endless ways of suggesting the sitter's character by the lines of his face, but before we set the windows of our house we make sure the foundations are solid and the walls well built. It is essential that the construction of the planes of a portrait be correct, and that the features are built into the general form of the head in their correct relation to it and to each other. Details are not so important as the basic construction. The quality that gives each face its own inherent character must be always sought for, but begin with the fundamentals and build from all angles, continually turning the model around and seeing it in every light.

To facilitate this building up, and to verify the relative sizes and placing of the features, it is sometimes advisable to take a set of measurements. These may be taken with a curved compass or calipers and set on paper in a life-sized diagram, for reference use; then they may be built up in the clay and a small point of wood about one inch long pushed into the clay to mark the spot, its tip left just above the surface.

One should bear in mind, from the outset, the material in which the portrait is finally to be made, for polished marble, stone, and bronze *all demand different treatments*. The hard resistance of Belgian black or Egyptian porphyry suggests a conventional simplification of style, while soft stone or bronze permits a more detailed and realistic manner of modeling.

The casting of a head in bronze will always cause a certain shrinkage in all dimensions—about three-sixteenths of an inch to a foot.

Terra cotta (after the clay is baked) shrinks one inch to a foot, and unless carefully prepared by an expert the terra cotta shell will shrink unevenly and cause serious deformations.

Suggestions to the Student for Modeling a Portrait

Begin by an erect position of the head; the pose may be changed afterwards if desired.

1. Leave enough space in front and all around the armature for freedom in modeling. Better too much than too little.

2. Prepare 40 or 50 rolls of well-kneaded clay.

3. Put clay on neck and cover pipe compactly with rather solid clay—not too soft.

4. From side view: build up line of profile, face, and head and neck.

5. Face the model: build up the widths of head.

6. Take the following measurements with curved calipers; set the screw after taking the distance on the model. Transfer these to a large piece of paper, so that they can be kept for future reference.

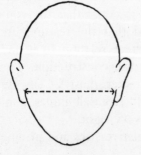

7. Take width between ears at   ; set matches 1″ long into clay so that ends are exactly like measurements on model. Gauge their position from front to back. Sometimes they are not exactly alike; one is often set higher on the head, or at a more acute angle, than the other. Note this carefully.

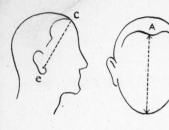

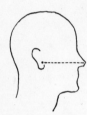

8. Set point A at correct distance up from chin point to where the hair begins to grow on forehead. Check this by describing an arc CC with calipers from each ear. When the arcs intersect and touch the distance point A, you will have your third dimension.

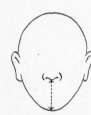

9. Set position of nose. Measure maximum distance from tip of nose to each ear. These measures may not be exactly equal. Set points in firm clay.

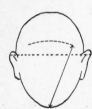

10. Set point at distance down to chin extremity from nose point and check this projection from each ear point, until they all click together.

11. Be sure all points are visible and steady before proceeding. Do not push them in until your head is completely constructed.

12. Describe arc with calipers, chin point to eyebrow level.
13. Maximum width from ear tip to ear tip.

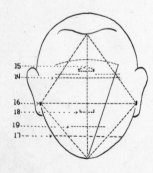

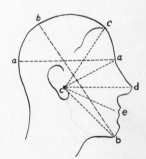

14. Width of outside limit of eyes.
15.   "   "   inside   "   "   "
16.   "   "   cheekbones.
17.   "   "   jawbone.
18.   "   "   nostrils.
19.   "   "   mouth.

138

103. *Amen-Hetep III, King of Egypt, About 1450 B.C., British Museum.*

104. *Caracalla, Vatican Museum, Rome.* (ALINARI)

105. *"The Baby Jesus,"* by Donatello, Florence. (ALINARI)

106. *Louise Brongniart, by Jean Antoine Houdon, The Louvre.*

(PHOTOGRAPHIC ARCHIVES OF ART AND HISTORY, PARIS)

108. *Bronze, Rodin Museum.*

107. *Terra Cotta Study, Metropolitan Museum.*

Balzac, by Rodin

109. *Final Version of Head for Full-length Figure.*

110. *Egyptian Sculpture, Granite Statue of Senmut Holding a Princess, 1470* B.C.

111. *Plaster Portrait of Camille Claudel, by Rodin.*

112. *"The Thought," by Rodin, Marble, Luxembourg Museum.*

113. *Portrait of Augustus Saint-Gaudens Modeling a Bas-relief, by Kenyon Cox, Metropolitan Museum.* (EWING GALLOWAY)

114. *Portrait of Joseph Hodges Choate, by Herbert Adams, Union League Club, New York.*

115. Abraham Lincoln, Portrait by Daniel Chester French in the Lincoln Memorial, Washington.

116. "Nan," by Jacob Epstein, Tate Gallery, London.

117. Giovanni Boldini, by Malvina Hoffman, 1928, Brooklyn Museum.

118. *Picasso, Carved in Stone, by Pablo Gargallo.*

119. *Maffio Maffü, by R. Romanelli.*

THE FIGURE

Before embarking on modeling a figure, the student should understand the main large planes that constitute the torso construction and the angles at which these planes turn into the next area. Innumerable drawings should be made from all angles to familiarize the student with the changes that take place in the torso alone, whenever there is a variation in position. When making these studies, the cross section shape should be kept in mind, as well as the profiles, and noted on the drawing. This will keep the three-dimensional quality growing in the artist's mind.

The main masses of the torso are affected by the bony and muscular structure of this region. The spine is the mainspring of all the movements, and its relation to the head and pelvic region should be carefully studied. The cage of the ribs has many variations in shape caused by the action of breathing. This bony cage is covered by the pectoral muscles in front, latissimus dorsi and external oblique on the sides, and the shoulder blades and their muscles, as well as the trapezius muscle, on the back. This last triangular-shaped muscle spreads out on both sides of the spine and rises to the shoulder blades (scapulae) and is attached as well to the neck, giving it great strength. Below the external oblique the gluteus medius and maximus form the buttocks. In front of the neck the sternocleidomastoid springs from the sternum and clavicle in two tendons on each side, forming the side supports of the neck and attaching itself behind each ear to the mastoid process at the base of the skull.

The shoulder joint is covered and heavily padded by the deltoid muscle. This has three sections, on which the arm is hung. The pectoral and triceps also serve to attach the arm to the upper body. The central section of the deltoid attaches itself to the upper arm bone between the triceps at the back and biceps on the front of the humerus. At its upper terminal the deltoid attaches to the scapula and clavicle. At the elbow joint the lifting action is done by the biceps, which start (under the front pad of the deltoid) on the upper humerus and attach below to the forearm between the supinator and pronator muscles. The upper tendon of the supinator has its attachment to the humerus, just below the deltoid attachment.

The articulation of the legs to the pelvic bone permits of a wide range of action. The bone of the upper leg is called the femur. The two bones forming the lower leg are the tibia (shinbone) and fibia (smaller bone inside it). The main hip muscle is the gluteus maximus and below this the

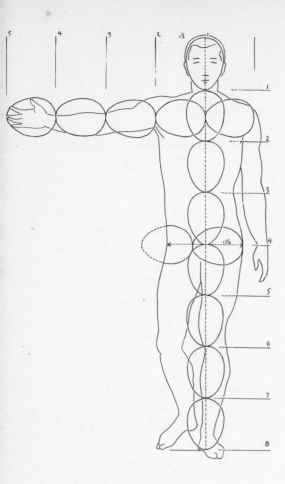

120. Diagram of Figure, Showing Relative Proportions.

121. Back View of Figure, Showing Proportion of Eight or Ten Heads to Length of the Figure.

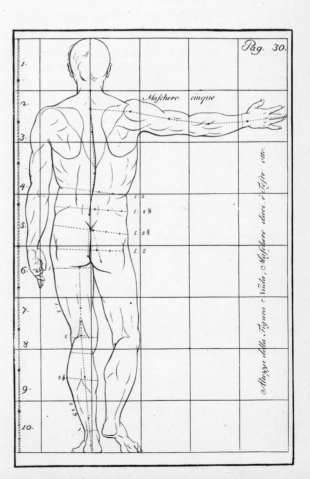

Pag. 30.

Mafchere cinque

Altezza della Figura e Nata, Mafchere dieci e Tefte otto.

vastus externus, which forms the outer contour of the upper leg seen from the front.

The patella, or kneecap, is held in place by tendons above and below, attaching it to the femur and tibia, or main bone, of the lower leg.

When building up the clay figure it is well to apply the clay in small pieces, carefully indicating the different planes and their boundaries. If these pieces are left without smearing, they give a fresh and definite idea of the anatomy of form. There is always plenty of time to pull them together and simplify the surface later on, when the construction is completed. If, on the contrary, the student rubs his fingers nervously over the surface while searching for the fundamental planes, it will be more difficult for him to determine the actual angles and limitations of his forms, and the result will be loss of time and a confused, troubled surface that gives no impression of anatomical security. Using small wire tools and picking at the clay should be avoided. The fingers alone, with one or two quite large tools, should suffice for all such constructional work.

It is well to start by building up the forms just a little smaller than the final surface will demand, for by so doing you will avoid having to cut off and remove surplus clay, and the whole figure will grow from the inside outward until completed.

It is essential to keep the whole idea of the figure, torso, head, arms, and legs, developing together as a unit. Do not push one section of the whole ahead of the others until the pose and essential lines of action and proportion are securely established. Try to locate the main lines of direction when the pose is selected; accent these, and beware of the fact that the model will often shift his weight imperceptibly while posing, which will completely alter these main lines of support and balance.

The sculptor must lock the original impression safely in his mind and use the model to carry out his idea. He must not try to copy too exactly what he sees, for he will find himself forever changing the forms and losing all the fresh definition of his original conception. Remember that models are human beings who feel fatigue in posing, just as you would if you ever tried it. Let them rest often, and do not abuse their patience or good will.

There are endless ways by which a sculptor can let the model rest an arm or a leg while he is concentrating on finishing some special area or working on the head. It is useful in action poses to have a rigid bar set on the wall of the studio so that the model can touch it while holding his pose on the stand. A rope hanging from the ceiling also serves as a useful support in difficult dancing or action poses.

122. *Torso by* Aristide Maillol, *Metropolitan Museum.*

123. *"Negro Dancing Girl," by the Negro Sculptor,*
Richmond Barthé. (ESTELLE WOLF)

When a model bears his weight on one leg, the ankle of this leg should be in direct plumb line with the pit of the neck. The shoulder over the relaxed leg is naturally higher than the one over the standing leg. The curve of the spine and instinct for balance are the cause of this.

Average Measurements for the Human Figure

7½-8 Heads = height of body.
2   "   = width of shoulder.
1½   "   =   "   " male hip.
2   "   =   "   " female hip.
1¼   "   = shoulder to elbow.
1¼   "   = elbow to tip of third finger.

The distance from a point in the center of brow to the tip of chin often equals the length of the hand.

The female skull is slightly smaller than the male. The shoulders are narrower, the arms shorter, the torso longer, and the legs shorter. The width at the waist is smaller and at the hips wider than in the male.

When a child is about three or four years old his height is about half the height of a man. At ten or eleven years he is three-quarters the height of a man.

When fully developed the weight of a man's muscles equals about half his entire weight.

DRAPERY

Clothing and costume depend largely on climate or the moral habits of the various races. Individual taste in the line of dress is generally controlled by rigid styles imposed by fashionable dressmakers. In the case of modern men, the imagination seems to have become so limited by custom that it can only vary between tropical shorts and the usual tailored suit. The evening seems to allow of more variety and play of personal fancy in the case of women, but in the male category, habit has restricted itself to a sort of international uniform of black cloth dinner coats or tails. What a relief we feel when traveling in the tropics to see the white evening mess jackets with their wide satin belts. At least the shape of the jacket is not identical with the cut of the regular dinner coat, with its black tie and stiff shirt front.

Gone, alas, are the days of pastel shades of beautiful Empire costumes,

124. Bronze Statuette of Athena, National Museum, Athens.

125. "Birth of Venus," Greek Sculpture, 5th Century B.C., *Museum of the Terme, Rome.* (ALINARI)

152

126. Drawing of Drapery by Michelangelo, British Museum. (ANDERSON)

when the long, tight-fitting trousers and the velvet, long-tailed coats added such elegance, when the distinguished high white stocks, billowing lace jabots, and ruffles of real lace gave the general effect of a "dandy"!

But to come to the serious problem of drapery in art. Like most things, drapery has its own laws and principles which must be studied and thoroughly understood before the student tackles it; he must not start with the idea that any lines modeled over the nude in vague folds and directions may serve to represent drapery.

When the nude figure is completed and well suggested in all its contours and planes, the lines of the drapery which you superimpose on the figure must be carefully chosen to accentuate just what you wish to emphasize in the pose of the figure.

You must select the main theme line of the drapery and then design the less important folds to compose with this main theme.

Every material may be suggested by different treatment in the modeling. The depths of the folds differ, and the actual design made by the heavy or light materials has a wide variety of possibilities.

It is useful to drape a few pieces of flannel cloth, muslin, and heavy satin over objects, or even hang them from nails on the wall, and from these make many careful drawings before even trying to model. Dampen these cloths and see what changes take place in the folds. There is hardly ever sufficient emphasis laid upon the necessity to draw before modeling. In bas-reliefs, above all, the design depends completely on the ability of the sculptor to draw his line with understanding and authority. In making a relief, the modeling tool is often used exactly like a pencil, accentuating and cutting a line on the background, or indicating, by a few essential, well-drawn lines, the exact turn of an edge or the placing of the muscles, or the direction of draped folds over a nude body.

If we study the wood carving by Ivan Meštrović with this particular matter in mind, we can easily realize how expert is his knowledge, his technique. Here is an artist so sure in draftsmanship that he uses his chisel as deftly as a duelist aims his rapier. Examine the extraordinary elimination of unessential details and see how the few selected lines, so carefully drawn, can indicate quite adequately a complete drapery with no obstructive complexities.

The deep folds naturally cast shadows on the nude, and these should indicate the form of the figure beneath the covering of drapery. They must never suggest that any line of the drapery has been cut into the actual surface of the nude figure. Sometimes the nude clay figure may be covered with a thin layer of muslin strips, so that when experimenting on the drapery the tool will strike the muslin, and the student will be warned of the fact that he must not cut deeper or he will be below the skin surface of the figure.

A good way to study movement in flying or fluttering drapery is to hang a chiffon scarf on some support and place an electric fan near by. The air will blow the light material in horizontal, waving folds. To make many drawings of such a changing problem is excellent practice before attempting to draw dancers on the stage, for instance. For the eye must be as swift as the movement of the dancer, and a subconscious knowledge of the laws of drapery makes it easier for the artist to suggest, by a few salient and essential lines, the design of the drapery which passes so swiftly before his vision.

During the seven years of my association with Anna Pavlowa, the greatest Russian dancer, I made innumerable studies of her in action on the stage. Sometimes I would be in the wings and sometimes in the audience. We would examine them together after the performance and decide which ones seemed to catch a movement accurately and which ones suggested the action just previous and just after the movement we wished to capture. By this method we collected about one hundred and fifty poses, from which we selected the twenty-five for the bas-relief frieze of "La Bacchanale."

From these drawings I made sketches in clay, in the round. Then I made reliefs two feet high of the whole series. Years later these were again enlarged to four feet in height and treated in a simpler manner than the small size.

The composition of drapery in such a series of panels presents as much of a problem as the modeling of the figures. For drapery in action is never the same, and the design must always be kept in harmony with the action of the figure. It is by the selection of movement in the floating drapery that we can sometimes suggest the action immediately previous or just to follow. It can serve to carry along the rhythm of our design and make it continuous as the music to which the figures may be dancing. The folds will indicate the tempo of the music and the speed of the action, as well as serving to fill the spaces between the figures with harmonious interest.

The student may feel that all this preliminary study is unnecessary and that there must be some short cut. *There is not.* The sincere, conscientious pupil will never tire of studying as long as he feels himself progressing either in understanding or in technique. When he suddenly realizes that he has grasped the principle of some difficult problem, he will be so encouraged that nothing will seem too long or too difficult to tackle. It will endow him with new courage and strength.

The eye of a fold—the form at the bend of a fold—must be higher in relief than elsewhere. The material is bent at this point, and every drapery, flannel, silk, leather, or velvet, has a varying angle at the eye. Arrange pieces of different quality on a board and study their individual characteristics, which repeat themselves in varying designs, but are always constructed on the same principles.

When modeling drapery on a relief, it must be drawn from the front view first and laid on the background in its definite pattern. Then it must be built up from the side views to give it the flow and variety of volume which is desired. It should also be studied from below, so that the sections at every point are correctly indicated. All this will give a sense of authority to the work.

It is important to locate the main points on the figure from which the drapery hangs. It is from these that the folds take their direction, and when studying which group of folds is to be the most important, it is wise to eliminate all others, which in most cases merely confuse or destroy the main structure of the design. If the artist succeeds in suggesting the drapery with a few fundamental lines, the effect is always more convincing, and the simple surfaces between the folds rest the eye and give emphasis to the groups of separated folds.

If we study the archaic period of art we find all complexities of drapery design simplified and reduced to an irreducible minimum, with striking success. The Egyptians certainly left plenty to the imagination of those who examined their work, never adding details when they were unnecessary, but always leaving sufficient material in the stone or porphyry for the eye and mind to feel the presence of the forms, without the sculptor having actually carved them.

This again is proof of a thorough understanding of the anatomy of drapery and form, as well as the physical anatomy of the human figure.

X. Carving

STONE CARVING

THE earliest drawings on stone and primitive carvings give undisputed evidence of artistic ability in the time of the cave dwellers. They designed ambitious compositions which included human beings, animals, and plant life, and a wide range of poses and actions.

Probably as the archaic designers grew bolder in their art experiments, they found that their drawings became more dramatic if the backgrounds were chipped away. And so, bas-relief came into being. This tempted the carvers to carry the idea of light and shadow still further by deepening the cuts and removing more of the background, making high relief. The early craftsmen soon found out not only how to make separate figurines in clay, but they discovered the means of baking this clay and hardening it; and after using sheets of metal to decorate their wooden carvings, they began to explore the possibilities of melting the metal and making casts. Later came the desire to reproduce the original objects, and the various methods of molds and lost-wax casting were developed. Carving tools have always been about the same: the point, the chisel, the pitching tool, the rasp, and the heavy mallet with its stubby metal head.

It would be well for students to understand why they should carve directly in stone while they are studying the first principles of sculpture. This *actual experience* will teach them more than weeks of argument or volumes of books. The resistance of the stone controls their minds; the appearance of forms as they emerge in the stone gives the carver a new demonstration of why the stone demands a solid form. Details and personal attributes are automatically subordinated to the basic needs of the material.

156

127. Carving Tools. Left to Right: 1. Pitching Tool. 2. Round-mouth Point (for Limestone or Soft Stone). 3. Point (for Marble). Toothed Chisels for Cutting Soft Stone or Marble.

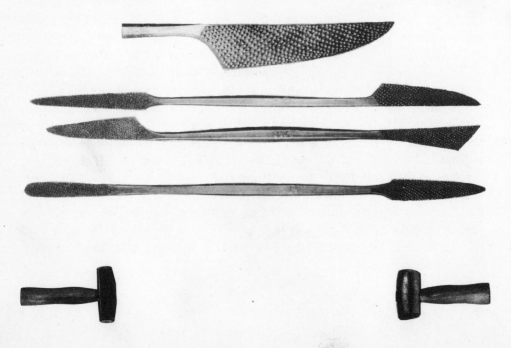

128. Steel Marble Rasps. Metal-headed Hammers.

Training that is limited to modeling in clay, for casting into bronze, is liable to lead the student into dangerous channels. He will probably become intrigued in the details of drapery, expression of the face, gestures of action, etc. The plastic consistency of clay is a temptation to model unessentials. There are, of course, important details which may be interpreted in bronze quite legitimately. The discipline which stone and marble impose upon the artist, however, is unquestionably the best teacher that a student could have. Stone is a taskmaster that is unprejudiced, that presents the same obstacles to every student, old or young, archaic or modern, that commands undivided attention and tenacity of purpose, strong, steady hands, and infinite patience.

The difficulty of a problem often improves the quality of its solution. When a sculptor has learned to animate stone and finds the means of expressing in simple, basic forms the symbol of his ideas, he has overcome the real dragon in the fight of his own development as a carver.

Such, then, is the safety device which may prevent the clay-modeling student from falling into a whole series of errors from which otherwise he would find no means of escape, unless some honest soul appeared to hit him on the head and set him on the right track—perhaps years after the student had become quite expert in modeling all kinds of intricate and useless details.

There is, in the very nature of stone itself, a more *sculpturesque* quality than in any other medium. It was this innate, enduring quality that lured the great sculptors to struggle against all its difficulties, because in the end they knew their work would have more solidity of form than ever could be achieved in metal.

Marble carving is a slow and tedious profession, demanding expert skill and accuracy. Very often the work is prepared by the "metteur au point," or "marble pointer," who takes off the surplus material to within an eighth of an inch or less of the finished surface; now the sculptor takes up the work and gives to the surface his individual texture and vibration of lights and shade. This "pointing" of marble is done with the assistance of a delicately adjusted pointing machine, which is hung on the original plaster at three points; by means of a steel needle the heights of the surface are all registered by hand and the needle set on an adjustable arm. The pointing machine is then transferred to the stone and hung on three points that correspond identically with those on the plaster model. The excess stone is cut away until within one-thirty-second of an inch of the final depth. A point hole is drilled carefully and marked just a fraction higher on the stone than on the model. The needle is gently pushed into this hole and the point

129. *Showing How Pointing Machine Is Hung on Original Plaster Model, the Needle Being Pushed Through Until It Touches the Surface Which Is Marked with a Pencil Point, the Set-screw Tightened with the Right Hand and Needle Drawn Back. The Machine Is Then Lifted Onto the Marble and Hung on Three Points Identically Placed as on the Original Model.*

130. *Showing How Long Drill Chisel Is Rolled Between the Palms of the Hands to Drill Into the Surface of the Marble to 1/32 of an Inch of the Exact Depth of the Pointer Needle. The Set-screw Shown Between the Hands and the Up-right Rod Determines the Distance That the Needle May Be Pushed.*

131. *Removing Surface Between Points with Tooth Chisel and Metal Hammer.*

checked. It is not unusual to take three or four thousand points to prepare a portrait for the final surface. If the machine shifts, or the needle is not accurately set, the entire effect will be ruined by errors in the pointing. (See page 170 for setting main points on stone.) Always proceed from highest points all over the model.

Rodin had a perfectly definite technique which is easily recognized. He told me that he had spent many hours studying Michelangelo's sculpture in Florence and identifying the strokes of certain tools, and just what effects they were capable of giving. His absolute modesty and self-effacement in the presence of these eternal masterpieces was one more proof of his true greatness.

Rodin's endless searching, day and night, was how to translate nature into a simple, continuous line; and the thousands of drawings, which I had the privilege of sorting and cataloguing, in 1919, will always be an instructive testimony of his indefatigable study.

When the subject in clay is destined to be carved in granite, the sculptor must study, before modeling, just what the limitations and demands of granite are, for it is a hard and relentless material, in which details and insignificant forms must all be eliminated.

In Tréguier, northern Brittany, there is a recent war memorial executed in the granite of the country. The figure is well adapted to the simple, large surfaces; in spite of the absence of detail—and in fact because of this—the massive design commands our reverence and respect for the subject. It is a revelation to sculptors to travel along the coast of Brittany and examine the numberless granite Calvaries and find the simplicity but richness of design that these native artists have achieved in their hard material. One of the most beautiful examples is at Plougastel, and dates from the year 1600.

When Belgian black marble or Herzegovinian black marble is used there is the possibility of developing the surface to appear grayish and rough by pointing, and then the surface can be chiseled to a mat-smooth finish. By rubbing with emery paper, the same marble can be given a highly polished surface of a deep velvety black. It can then be finished by rubbing with pumice powder and oil until the surface shines like a mirror.*

It is interesting and instructive to note just how good workmen move and handle heavy stones. There is no waste motion, no nervousness; a thorough knowledge of balance and an intelligent margin for safety are always taken into their calculations. If you *do* learn from experts, it will save you many a strained back, a pinched finger, or even a serious accident caused by ignorance of handling.

* The actual sequence of polishing includes: 1. Fine emery stone; 2. Coarse sandstone; 3. Fine sandstone; 4. Pumice stone; 5. English hone; 6. Putty powder and powdered oxalic acid on dampened rag; 7. Rub until you give out! Wash stone with clean water and clean rag between each operation.

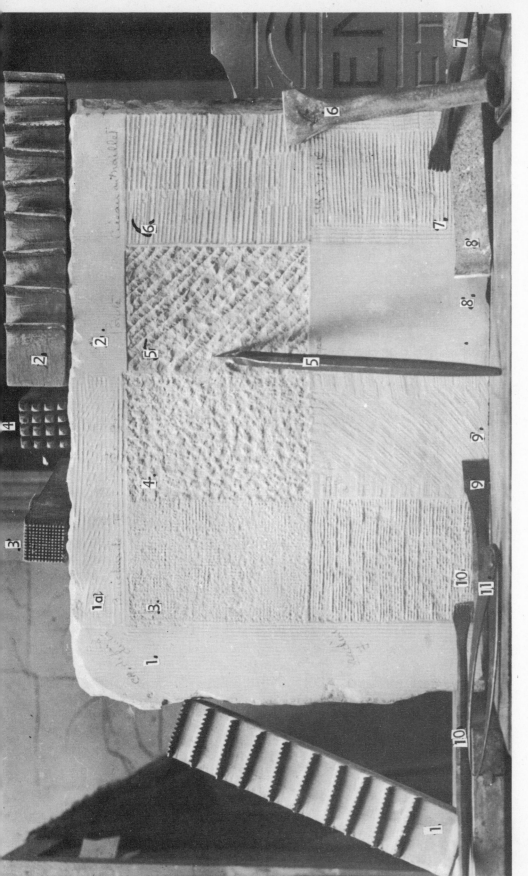

132. *Showing Various Surfaces Produced on Stone by the Use of the Tools Bearing the Numbers of the Different Sectors:* 1. French-toothed Scraper Rough, Drawn Straight. 1A. French-toothed Scraper Rough, Crossed. 2. Smooth Scraper. 3. Fine-toothed Bush Hammer. 4. Rough-toothed Bush Hammer. 5. Pointer. 6. Large Flat Chisel. 7. Flat-toothed Chisel. 8. Curved Flat French Tool with Sharp Edge Pushed Over the Surface. 9. Medium-width Flat Chisel. 10. Finer-toothed Flat Chisel. 11. Compass.

I once had a painful but useful lesson myself when finishing one of my first marble portraits. The head and neck were completed but the base seemed to need leveling; the head was laid on its back on a wooden stand, without sufficient padding under it or enough support under the neck. Striking the chisel against the base a bit too strenuously caused the marble to fracture, and the finished head suddenly broke off and fell to the floor, breaking off a tip of the ear as well. This tragedy at the start was such a shock that the lesson will never be forgotten. I pass on this incident merely to warn others to leave a section of solid marble at the back of the neck until the end and see that your base is perfect before you finish all the work on the head.

In spite of precautions, accidents are bound to happen, for sculpture is a series of hazards, and even when the work is safely finished and accepted, the packing and shipping of sculpture is another task requiring great skill and intelligence. Packers often omit to fasten sufficiently padded yokes or braces inside the case to prevent the work from shifting during its transportation. In the case of a bust, for instance, the head and neck are generally far lighter in weight than the shoulders or base. The padded yoke should be fitted over the heaviest section and securely screwed into the sides of the strong case before the firm wads of excelsior are wedged in every part of the empty areas. Cases are pulled about by truckmen with hooks and left to fall over by their own weight. They are pushed into steep chutes from steamers and bumped violently against other cases. No matter what the red signs or stamped warnings may say, in any language, freight is freight and that to sculptors means fright and damage.

Insurance values are a game of their own, and when a head is broken off a marble, the company agents have generally a very different idea of the extent of loss than the poor devil who has carved the work and lost his year's rent by the accident.

The United States has a fine supply of stone, granite, and marble quarries. The stone most generally used in city buildings is known as Indiana limestone. Buildings are often based upon a foundation of granite. If the building is to be of white marble, the State of Georgia supplies a fine product for this purpose. Colorado Yule is another type of white marble.

Certain buildings, such as the Morgan Library in New York and the new Mellon Gallery in Washington, for example, are built of Tennessee marble. This is a slightly mottled, creamy beige color. The Public Library in New York is made of marble from Vermont. There is also a limestone quarry in Alabama, the stone from which is widely used for buildings.

133. Clear White Carrara Marble Quarry, Italy. (COURTESY OF THOMPKINS KIEL)

134. Alabama Marble Quarry. (COURTESY OF THOMPKINS KIEL)

135. *Stone and Marble Yard, Leger &
Son, Paris.* (BERNES MAROUTEAU)

136. *Sawing Marble Slab. Disk of
Carborundum Revolves at High Speed.
Water Is Kept Flowing Over the Sur-
face. The Operation Is Guided at the
Wheel by Mr. Leger.*
(BERNES MAROUTEAU)

137. *Revolving Carborundum Disk for
Polishing Marble Slabs, Guided by Mr.
Leger.* (BERNES MAROUTEAU)

138. Rounding the Moldings of a Pedestal. Tool Is Braced Against Block and Held Against Revolving Marble Base.
(BERNES MAROUTEAU)

140. Machine Used to Hollow Out Stone and Marble Jars and Bowls. Water Runs Through Tube Into Cavity to Cool the Grinding Core Drill.
(BERNES MAROUTEAU)

139. Marble Cube Being Rubbed and Polished on a Revolving Grinding Wheel. Sand and Water Flow Over the Surface, and Model Must Be Pressed Down Firmly to Ensure Square Corners and Flat Surface. (BERNES MAROUTEAU)

Tombstone carving is generally done in Vermont or New Hampshire granite. These are both very durable out of doors. Vermont also supplies a mottled white marble, Maryland and Connecticut greens of varied tone and veining. The white marble of Georgia has certain streaks in it, but in Alabama the white marble is clear and suitable for figure carving.

The Italian marbles known as Carrara and Serravezza are pure crystalline white and ideal for figure carving to be placed indoors. Pentelic Greek marble has always been a very popular white marble.

There are softer stones in France of lovely warm tones of beige and pink which lend themselves to figure carving for inside work with fine effects. The granite of Brittany is a dour gray and a challenge to any carver's strength and patience.

141. "Javanese Girl," Malvina Hoffman, Bl Belgian Marble.

(BERNES MAROUTEA▮

CLEANING STONE

High-pressure steam can be used to clean stone monuments, but sand-blasting should not, because it destroys surface details.

Great harm can be done to stone carvings if the cleaning is not done by reliable experts. If the surface is brushed over with acid and then sprayed with steam pressure, the result is often startlingly good; but if this newly cleaned surface is not thoroughly gone over with a neutralizing wash to stop any further action of the acid, which has been forced into the pores by the pressure of steam, there will be a gradual discoloration and injury to the surface of the stone which only makes itself evident a long time afterwards.

A great deal of research and constructive work has been done in this direction by the Monument Restoration Project, under the direction of the Department of Parks and Mr. Karl Gruppe, the sculptor, who devoted five years to this work and is responsible for this project.

As a timesaving device—and time seems to be worth even more than money these days—when large surfaces are to be cut on stone the modern carver often uses a pneumatic hammer which is attached to a long rubber tube. The compressed air is forced through this tube and a metal holder containing the hammer, and causes a chisel to vibrate up and down at a high rate of speed when its tip is pressed against the stone surface. This tool must be held steadily in both hands and guided with expert skill.

TEMPERING AND SHARPENING CARVING TOOLS

Place the end of the steel tool in the red coals of a blacksmith's forge (soft blacksmith coal and charcoal mixed). Do not push the tool deep into the fire. If you burn the steel it will fall to pieces when put under a strain. Watch the tool very carefully so it does not overheat; it must be cherry red. Lift it out by tongs and hold it over the anvil. Hammer and shape it on the anvil after heating in fire.

After the tool, for example one-quarter-inch steel, is shaped, replace it in the fire. Take it out when the tip is cherry red. At this point dip the tool to one-half inch into cold water, and count three slowly. Rub it quickly on a sand board to see the temper.

The tip should be white, blending into gold, turning into bronze, turning into purple, turning into blue as it goes up the shaft of the tool. (These colors do not show until the hot tool has been dipped in water and rubbed on sand.) The temper should only color the tool for about three-quarters to one inch above the tip. As the tool cools to the desired color, dip it immediately in cold water again to hold the temper.

For marble, the color should be bluish purple. Bronze or golden tempers are used for granite carving.

The harder the tool is tempered the quicker it will break when struck against hard stone or granite. Tooth chisels may be hammered until they cool off, and then their teeth may be filed. Finishing chisels may be tempered hard, because they are used only for surfaces and not for splitting or cutting.

Solution of brine for tempering granite-carving tools: about one-half pound of rock salt to five gallons of water.

When carving a figure, the sculptor always keeps a piece of wet, soft stone for rubbing his tools whenever they become dull.

The iron-headed hammer, for roughing out, should weigh about three to four pounds; for finishing, a two-pound hammer is adequate.

Do not hold the chisel too straight over the stone. It must be held at an angle so that the edge bites the surface but does not dig into the stone and chew up the surface. Drills turned by a wire bow may be used for deep places when tools cannot safely be used.

142. War Monument Carved in Granite by Francis Renaud, Tréguier, Brittany.

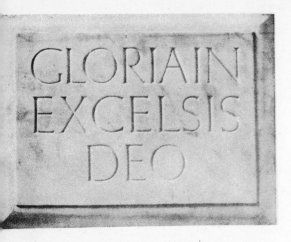

143. *V-cut Type of Lettering, Carved in Marble. Designed by Percy Smith.*

144. *Example of Letters Flush with Surface of Stone on Sunken Background. Designed by Percy Smith.*

145. *"Sculpture" Shows Raised Type of Lettering, High Relief, Straight Edges.*

146. *"Inside and Out," V-cut Into Surface of Stone.*

147. Method for Establishing Main Points on a Stone. Plaster Model on the Right. Stone to Be Same Size as the Model.

METHOD FOR ESTABLISHING MAIN POINTS ON A STONE

Model to be Reproduced in Same Size and Proportions

Buy the stone with plenty of surplus for safety.

Be sure to put two marks on model indicating the correct plumb line.

1. Lay model on its back. Set points 1, 2, 2*a*, and 3 on its base. Lay stone face up on the ground and establish its base line to correspond exactly with the base of the plaster model.

2. Square off the bottom bed of stone on which it is to stand when finished. Set points 1, 2, 2*a*, and 3 in same relation as these points are set on model.

3. Draw a straight line two or three inches above the actual limit edge of stone base and set these points on this line. Set base points of machine on 1 and 2.

4. Locate highest point on top surface of model point 4. Set this 1″ in projection from surface. Square up on model from base, one angle of square tight against base area, other angle over point 4. Measure distance from inside of square edge to this point for depth. Repeat this operation on stone. Set needle over point 4 and drill in to within ½″ of the final depth measure. Set straight pin on machine to this depth with setscrew.

Now your machine has three resting points: 1, 2, and 4. Check 4 in relation to 3 on model and stone by setting needle point on arm Y and Z.

5. Extend bar X with extension section and locate point 5 with long needle, leaving always a little surplus stone for safety.

These points must be perfect before proceeding with the work. On point 4 of model set nail. Bend head upward and put hole in center of head. This will become the hanging point 4*a* for machine when figure is set upright for later pointing.

Replace needle at point 5 with long, straight pin and set with setscrew on bar X. Set nail with bent-up head on point 5 of model to serve as another hanging point 5*a* for machine when work is set upright later on.

6. Set point 6 on top of head of model, with hole in center of a nail head allowing 1″ extra (hanging point later). Shift needle bar up to top of extended shaft of machine and locate point 6 on stone. Set long pin B with curved tip, with setscrews, on shaft X.

7. Replace needle arm at lower level to enable needle to locate points 7 and 8. Points 6, 7, and 8 form another triangle for hanging another smaller (30″, for example) machine.

8. To establish point 9 reset needle arm to position O and set needle to point 9 on model and drill into stone to same depth. Set bent nail on model at this point, head upward, for future hanging point for smaller machine.

9. It is readily seen how, from these accurately located main points, all other points on the model may be determined by following the same procedure. If any of the main points are incorrect, all the subsequent pointing will be inaccurate.

It is essential to study thoroughly and experience this work on an experimental basis before embarking on a serious project of carving.

This example only explains a reproduction of the model in stone of the same dimensions. When the model is to be enlarged in the stone every measurement must be exactly scaled off and set in correct proportion to the increased scale. This is a labor of infinite patience and exactitude and must be checked and rechecked with compasses throughout the operation by a conscientious craftsman. After all the areas are safely pointed, taking great care to place *all points ⅜″ full on the highest forms* all over the figure *8″ or 10″* apart, the surplus stone is cut off in large planes. Never take any finish points on any of the lower or deeper areas until all the heavy surplus stone has been removed and full points all verified.

Then proceed with finish points, but, for safety, *never set needle hard on the model*, but see light between the point and the surface of model. On the stone, cut away until the needle is hard on the stone, drill a little hole 1/16″ deep, and mark it with a pencil dot.

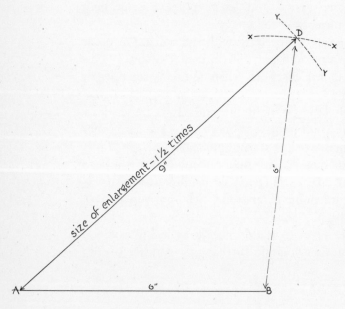

SCALE FOR ENLARGING 1½ TIMES
(*drawing 1″ to 1′ scale*)

Set caliper X for 6″ and caliper Y for 9″ which is 1½ times larger. Draw straight line A-B. Place caliper X on point A and describe an arc across line A-B. Place caliper X on point B and describe an arc X above line A-B. Place caliper Y on point A and cross arc X. At intersecting point D draw a straight line to point A.

Directions:

1. If ratio is less than twice, then measure off only *once* the size of model on line A-B before describing arc X.

2. If the ratio is over twice the size of model, but less than three times, you must measure this off twice on line A-B-C, before describing arc X.

3. For each additional ratio you must measure the distance on A-B as many times as you are enlarging the model, and follow same procedure for each measurement. The distance from intersecting points of arcs on line A-D to A gives proportional measurements for your enlargement.

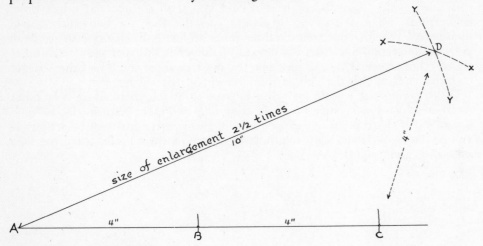

FOR ENLARGING 2½ TIMES

Set one caliper at 4″ and another at 10″ which is 2½ × 4″. Draw a straight line A-C. Place caliper X on point A and cross line A-C at point B. Then place caliper X on point B and again cross line A-C at point C. Now place caliper X on point C and describe an arc X-X above line A-C. Place caliper Y on point A and describe an arc Y-Y. At intersecting point D draw a straight line to point A. All measurements must be taken in the same order. Distances from A to points where arcs intersect line A-D give enlarged measurements.

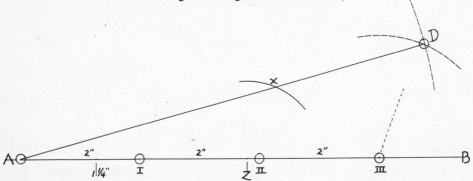

FOR ENLARGING 3½ TIMES

To establish scale measure of three times 2″ on line A-B describe 2″ arc from III above line A-B. Set second compass 3½ times 2 (or 7″), one point on A, and describe arc which intersects the first arc at D. At this point of intersection draw straight line to A.

X = foot to knee (for example, this measurement on small model equals 1¼″). Place caliper on A and measure this distance three times on line A-B and describe arc upward from this point Z intersecting line A-D. Place point of caliper on intersection point X and stretch other point to A. This will give you the distance of foot to knee on the enlargement.

If small-model measurement is 2′ 2″ and you wish a three and a half times enlargement, make a drawing to scale 1″ to the foot for convenience, and measure off 2″ with your compass three times on line A-B. Describe an arc from point 3 intersecting line A-D. Place point of caliper at this spot and stretch other leg of caliper to A. This will give you the distance three and a half times larger than the small model, the desired measurement of the enlargement.

When laying out a scale on wood be sure to attach strips of zinc or other metal on which you scratch your measuring lines and exact point marks, as wood is soft and if sharp point of caliper sinks in, all measurements will be wrong. If you set tacks on stone, with fine hole in center of their heads, make the hole as small as a pin point.

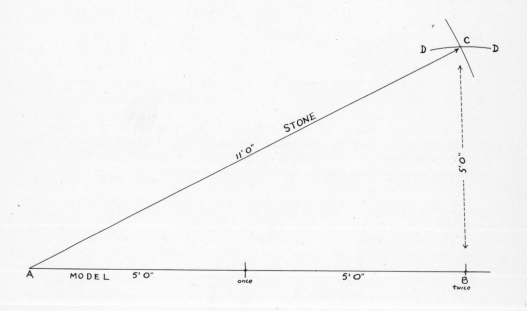

OPEN SCALE

For example, the model is 5 feet high, and sculptor has a block of stone 11 feet high to which he would like to enlarge his model. To establish the scale for this work he measures off the size of his model, which is 5 feet, twice on the line A-B and takes this same distance and describes an arc D-D. He sets other caliper at 11 feet and describes an arc from A, intersecting the arc D at C. From this point he draws a straight line to A. The angle thus formed between his base line A-B and the line A-C establishes the correct scale for his enlargement.

Any measurement taken on his model must be measured off on line A-B twice, and an arc of this same length described above it intersecting line A-C. The distance from this last intersection point to A gives him the corresponding measure for his enlargement.

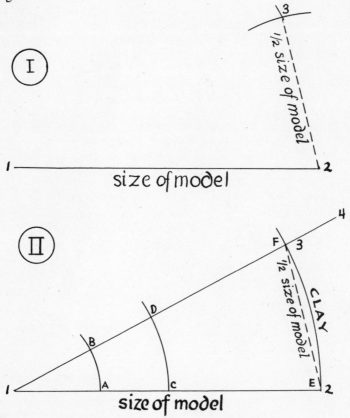

SCALE FOR ENLARGING UP TO TWICE THE SIZE OF ORIGINAL ONLY AND ALL SIZES IN REDUCTION

Diagram 1 shows ½ reduction. From 2 describe arc radius equal to ½ size of model. Then line 2 to 3 is the height of clay figure to be made. Diagram 2. Describe arc from 1 radius equal to size of model (1 to 2); this intersects arc of Diagram 1 (at 3) through which point draw line 1 to 4. All model measurements are marked off on line 1-2. From point 1 describe arcs at these various points to intersect line 1-4. A straight-line distance between intersecting points A-B, C-D, E-F will be proportionate measures for clay, one-half size of model.

148. *"Je Suis Belle," by Rodin.* (BERNES MAROUTEAU)

149. *A. J. J. Ayres, English Sculptor, Carving Stone on Outside of London Building.* (THE LONDON "TIMES")

150. *"The Sower," by Eric Gill. Soft Stone Model on Right of Full-size Figure.* (HOWARD COSTER)

151. *Bainbridge Copnall, English Sculptor, Working on Tubular Scaffolding, Finishing Stone Figure on Adelphi Building, London.* (UNIVERSAL PHOTOS)

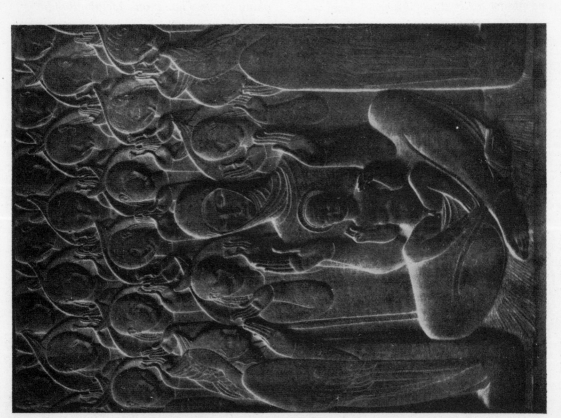

153. *Bainbridge Copnall Carving Wooden Figures.*

152. *"Madonna and Angels," by Ivan Meštrović.*

WOOD CARVING

If we could trace back the course of our development through the years and discover the incidents or accidents which left their mark upon us, we should find a great variety of unsuspected influences at work upon the loom of our destiny. The multicolored threads of life are woven into strange patterns. Long spaces seem to occur without any active design or vivid colors; then, suddenly, a streak of darkness gathers and the background of storm is torn with jagged flashes. The Great Designer has broken the gray monotony and keyed us up into a higher capacity of experience. We are often amazed at the sudden inrush of unexpected adventure; our pulse is speeded up; we feel a new awareness. A veil seems to be lifted from our eyes; we perceive and feel more keenly the existence of ourselves and others. Frequently it is the casual and apparently unimportant remark which leaves its stamp on our memory.

When I was about ten years old in Little Boar's Head, New Hampshire, Mr. Bennett Nash, professor of classic languages, introduced me to the delicate art of carving driftwood, with a penknife and homemade tools, into canoes and rowing shells fitted with seats, rowlocks, oars, rudders, and all the correct details of the tiny craft. He made me try out the tools on the rough bits of driftwood which we selected on our walks along the seashore. The upper stretches of sand near Big Boar's Head seemed to be our best hunting ground. He would tell me about the grain of the different woods and how carefully they were selected by shipbuilders.

My first effort was to make a little jewel box for mother, fitted with trays and drawer and lined with suède. Professor Nash took infinite pains to show me just how to miter the corners, countersink the hinges, and sandpaper every edge, even though these were to be covered by the leather lining. "Remember, Mallie, that the Japanese craftsmen stand out above others because of the perfection of their workmanship. They even carve the underside of bases and boxes, where only a few eyes ever discover their hidden, delicate designs. We Americans forget that the angels can see through and around and under just as well as from the front." This remark sank into my young mind and has been a constant guide and help to me throughout the years.

A good introduction to carving is for the novice to start in learning the handling of sharp tools by making simple forms in wood. A few steel chisels

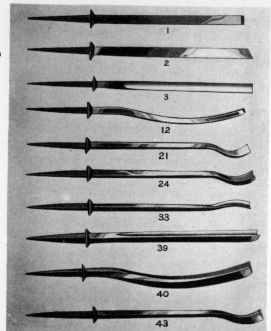

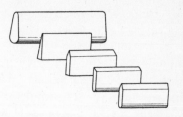

155. Slips for Sharpening Wood-carving Tools. These Are Shaped to Fit the Various Angles and Curves of the Blades.

154. Wood-carving Tools: 1. Chisel. 2. Skew Chisel. 3. Straight Gouge. 12. Long Bent Gouge. 21. Spoon Chisel. 24. Spoon Gouge. 33. Back Bent Gouge. 39. Straight Parting Tool. 40. Long Bent Parting Tool. 43. Spoon Parting Tool.

and gouges, a wooden mallet, a sharpening oilstone, and a block of wood held firmly in a vise on a heavy worktable—these are all the equipment necessary. Constant practice is the only way one can grow proficient in any branch of sculpture, and the hands must become strong and sure when directing the sharp cutting edge of a carver's tools.

Care must be taken to select good-quality handles on the chisels and gouges, for these must not slip in the hand, and they should be long enough to hold firmly without danger of striking the hand with the mallet. The ordinary type of octagonal handle for the larger tools is very satisfactory and not expensive.

For the smaller tools, a shorter polished handle is more comfortable. The index finger touches the top of the gouge, and the butt of the handle is held in the palm and pushed without the need of a mallet. The hardest and best mallets are made of lignum vitae, the heavy chisel handles of ash, which gives a certain amount of spring to the blow.

The oilstone slips (about 3 or 4 inches long) needed for sharpening the gouges are made in sizes and curves to fit the inside of the tools.

To sharpen tools properly, the carver must have a grindstone on which to grind off broken edges or superfluous metal. Great care must be taken at this stage to have a long, tapered bevel on the back of the tool, not a short, steep one like a carpenter's chisel.

The edges must be kept sharp as a razor blade. After grinding they must be rubbed on the oilstone on both sides. The edge must be straight, not jagged, and this applies to gouges as well as chisels. Even if the corners are slightly rounded off, all parts should be made equally sharp.

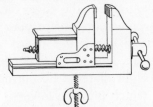

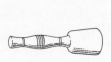

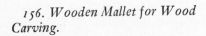

156. Wooden Mallet for Wood Carving.   *157. Vise for Wood Carving.*

The curved slips are rubbed inside the gouges, and it is easy to cut the fingers during this operation. Hold the tool in the left hand and rub the stone against the blade with the right hand. Do not fasten the stone and rub the tool against it: the results will not be so good. To finish the treatment the carving tools should be stropped like a razor on an ordinary barber's strop, always kept near by while working. If stropped often, the edge will be kept in good condition for a much longer time without need of oilstones.

Get a block of soft pine wood and try the edges by cutting across the grain. It seems difficult to believe, but some chisels will cut hard wood and yet will not cut soft wood in a clean way.

The beginner would do well to use pine or American whitewood. American walnut is of medium hardness. Mahogany—the Spanish variety—is very hard and darker in tone. Sandalwood, apple, and cypress are hard and close-grained, and this texture often gives a beautiful effect when rubbed and finished. The Indian sandalwood has a very pungent odor. Teak, ebony, and boxwood are also used for carving.

The vise, or "chops," to hold the wood must not wobble, and the bench must be heavy and firm. The wood to be carved must be shifted to different angles and positions to facilitate the work, but if held in cork- or leather-lined jaws, it will always be firm and uninjured by the pressure of the vise. A bench screw is very useful. It goes up through a hole in the bench and screws into the base of the block to be carved. A thick washer between the bench and the screw is a convenience and prevents wearing away the table when tightening the screw into position.

Cramps or thumbscrews are useful to clamp a board to the bench if it is to be carved into a relief.

A good way to begin wood carving is to draw a simple pattern on the wooden surface and cut the background away for an even depth to within a short distance of the design with gouges and mallet; this will establish the maximum height of your relief. Then follow the outline with chisels, practicing to cut the edges cleanly, and experiment with all the tools until they become obedient to your will.

Then take a larger board and draw on the design of your figure or drapery in definite, clear-cut lines. Proceed as before to establish the maximum height of relief by cutting away the background. Select the different planes which must be lowered from the maximum height, and lower them, taking care not to tear or split the wood surfaces. Remember that the angle at which you cut the outline will determine the value of light that will flow along the edge; and if your drawing is good, the slightest difference in planes will be sufficient to suggest the modeling, by slightly curving the surface as it meets the next plane's edge of light.

Only by your own experiments and experience will you become capable of getting your desired effects.

XI. Garden and Architectural Sculpture

SCULPTURE IN GARDENS

THE subject of pools and fountains has always been very close to my heart. Gardens have always seemed to me to be places of repose, refreshment, and romance. The fountain, with its delicious sound and ever-changing, crystalline beauty, has frequently been used as a symbol of spiritual and aesthetic thought.

We know of a Babylonian water basin found at Tello, dating back to 3000 B.C., and the early Assyrians used to catch their natural springs in hollowed stone basins, often one over another in a sort of cascade. On the lower one would be cut decorative bas-reliefs of lions. In the olden days fountains were often dedicated to the gods and heroes. A spring or pool determined the location of the sacred groves of Apollo and other deities. Herodotus mentions a fountain of Pyrene at Corinth, made of white stone, the ruins of which still remain. Horses, dolphins, and Poseidon often figured as decorations in the Greek fountains.

The legends of the Celts in Brittany and Cornwall tell us of superstitions and deep-rooted belief in the magical properties of fountains. Some in Cornwall are protected by Gothic vaults, and churches have been built near by. We are all familiar with the Italian primitives of the Virgin and Child, picturing them near a fountain.

Medieval gardens had many bathing pools, and very often we find bird baths, sculptured basins, and sundials. Sometimes an empty place on the side of a house was decorated with a wall sundial with very good results. The armillary sphere with the signs of the zodiac also lent itself to fine artistic treatment.

158. Ideal Combination of Architecture, Sculpture, and Garden Decoration. Giulio Richard, Architect, Milan.

The study of scale and proportion in a garden is especially necessary when placing a piece of sculpture either as a fountain figure or as the point of interest at the end of a path. It is vital that the figure be of the correct size and scale to fit the surroundings. The effect is often entirely spoiled by the lack of this very essential quality of good proportion. The best and safest way to avoid such errors is to try an enlarged photograph of the sculpture, mounted on plywood and held upright by a brace at the back. If this is done and, if possible, colored to resemble bronze or stone, the correct proportion can easily be obtained before the full-size figure is made by the sculptor.

If landscape architect and sculptor would study the problems together, instead of working independently of each other, as they so frequently do, we should have many better results in our American gardens.

The beauty of a reflection in a pool is always a source of pleasure. In the Orient and Persia especially, the designers of gardens and fountains frequently depend on this added attraction to their picture. Where water can be used, it is sure to add great charm and delight. It must, however, be used with discretion and study, as an element of gaiety or of peaceful reflection.

The basins and borders of pools are important parts of a fountain design. It is not the sculptured figure alone that is necessary. We must consider the paths of approach, the view from far and near, the planting around it, the proportion of the basin to the figure, and the height and bulk of its pedestal.

When building a wall, one should decide if a niche or archway would relieve monotony. In this niche a figure is often needed, but the color, size, and sentiment expressed are all important considerations. Here again, one should experiment with an enlarged photograph whenever possible. So often Americans going abroad to hunt antiques come upon a relic in stone or marble, or even bronze and lead, and buy it for their new garden. It is often difficult to find the right spot for these statues, and they generally look out of place unless the setting is carefully adapted to their special needs.

In wooded allees the occasional stone caryatid, satyr, or faun, half covered with ivy, such as we frequently meet in old French gardens, comes as a pleasant surprise.

One can have a garden without flowers, and having flowers does not always constitute a garden. Trimmed allees, walks, fragrant flowering shrubs, and shady trees around a refreshing pool, soft grassy glades or terraces— these form the main structure of a garden. Then, and then only, come the

159. Unusually Fine Architectural Treatment of a Natural Setting. Private Park Near Milan, Giulio Richard, Architect.

flowers, not too crowded, to add their special glory to the scheme. The plan of a garden is as important as the plan of a house.

Gardens all on one level soon become dull and lack surprise and variety. A terrace or a few steps can save this situation.

Greens, such as the darkest ivy and junipers, cedars, and pines, must be used to bring out the color and charm of flowers. Otherwise the orchestra of color without double basses will be empty and thin in tone. We must create mystery and suggest repose and spiritual refreshment, or we shall have clipped our garden of its wings.

If we can place a beautiful figure in marble against dark trees, or a bronze group in a stone niche of correct proportions, we can be sure that such a decoration will add great charm to any garden and give life and vibration to the entire composition.

160. "Nymph and Satyr," by Edward McCartan.

(LOUIS DREYER)

161. *Sun Dial by Brenda Putnam.*

162. *"Faun," by Paul Dardé, Colossal Lead Figure in Garden of Eugene Rudier, Le Vésinet Near St. Germain.*

163. *"St. Francis and His Animal Friends," Bronze, by Malvina Hoffman, Collection of Miss Anne Morgan.* (MATTIE EDWARDS HEWITT)

164. Bronze Gateway to the Bronx Zoological Garden, Paul Manship, Sculptor.
(DE WITT WARD)

*165. Proposed Lighting Effect of the International Dance Fountain by M. H.,
for the New York World's Fair, Rendering by Georg Hartmann.*

ARCHITECTURAL SCULPTURE

Knowledge of perspective and the principles of architecture should be part of a sculptor's mental equipment, for he should be able to read and visualize at a glance any plan or elevation of a garden or building. He should be able to draw, and render his proposed sculpture in a professional manner, showing its relation to the surroundings and including its base or pedestal.

This last subject is often the cause of much argument and many head-aches. The proportion and taste of a pedestal, or even a small wooden base, may add or detract seriously from the figure or portrait of which it is an integral part.

The art of presentation is too often neglected, both in the intimate small-sized bronzes and in the more formal decorative type of sculpture, in relation to size, material, and color; the bases should be carefully constructed to enhance the beauty of the object they are meant to set off to better advantage. When the two are correctly combined the results seem to click and appear inevitable.

The artist would do well to give himself constant memory tests in gauging distances, heights, etc., so that when he is confronted with a proposed site he can calculate accurately the size and proportions of the sculpture needed, or the distances from which the group, figure, or medallion will be seen.

How few people who build houses are ever able to read architectural blue-prints intelligently! And of how much pleasure they deprive themselves by just this inability to visualize their proposed home! Many arguments and disappointments would be avoided if the client had realized just what the size of "6′ x 8′" for his dressing room had really meant on the blueprint. How tiny and crowded the ocean liners' staterooms often seem, even though they were so carefully selected on the clever ship's plan booklet. Practice, pace it off and train your eye, and save yourself many a hard knock in life.

The tricks that high buildings play on us! The unbelievably huge scale that is demanded when carvings are set on a great exterior façade, since they would be lost and ridiculous if made too small! Notice the size of the little figure of Mercury stopping the traffic on every street lamp of Fifth Avenue, and see if he fits his job or his pedestal. Try to guess the diameter of Atlas's globe by Lee Lawrie in Rockefeller Center, and then consider the problem of making such a figure and balancing the great rings! The transporting and

166. *The Temple of Opet, Karnak, Egypt.*

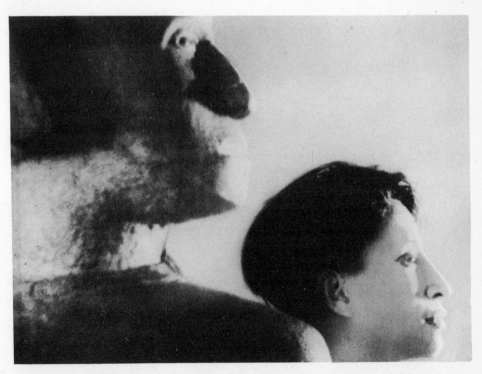

167. *Ancient Sculpture on a Mayan Temple, Living Type of Mayan, 1935.*
Note Striking Similarity of the Head Structure and Line of Profile.

(FROM FILM, "THUNDER OVER MEXICO")

168. "Chariot of the Moon," Angkor Vat, Indo-China.

assembling of this monumental group alone would make your own daily problems fade into insignificance.

When figures are to be placed seventy or ninety feet above the sidewalk —over a doorway, for instance—did you know that to appear erect they must be set tipped slightly forward, and that unless they are set on a rising base you would not be able to see their feet? If they are cut in stone, adequate ballast of material must be left at the back to counterbalance their tipping forward. Here again the enlarged photograph of a small model can be set up in place and judged for scale before deciding on the full size.

When carving a group to be seen on a building, it is important to know if the sun will shine upon it or whether only a north light will be on the work when in its permanent position. The carving of bas-reliefs or lettering must be deeper and more accentuated if to be seen without sunlight, for the details of low relief fade out in a north light, and from a distance much of the pattern or lettering becomes unreadable. The sun of course sharpens the high lights and intensifies the shadow values.

The higher up on a building that a relief is set, the deeper must be the undercuts. If reliefs are set on each story of a building, and are to appear as a uniform series of designs when seen from the sidewalk below, each one must be carved in higher relief than the one below. (See illustration of Copnall's reliefs.)

I recall visiting the sculptor MacMonnies in his garden at Giverny in France; he was placing one of his bronze figures on the high garden wall. He explained that the best way to test the strength and solidity of a piece of sculpture is to set it up on a wall against the sky. The test is a cruel one, but useful because one can quickly determine which profile silhouette holds its own against the blue infinity.

Another infallible test that he resorted to when his own judgment became fogged with fatigue was to ask a stranger on the street to come to his studio. He would turn his statue around slowly, and wait for the stranger to tell him which view he thought was the best. Invariably, MacMonnies told me, the visitor with his fresh eye would select the best and condemn the other views as being inferior, and he could resume his work with more conviction.

It is well to bear in mind that everything looks much smaller and less impressive when seen in the open air than when it is being worked up in a studio and seen within four walls generally lighted from a single source. When the model is taken out of doors and set up in a garden or on a large building, its size diminishes and we are confronted with the fact that what we felt was so important indoors is hardly noticeable in the enveloping light of day. Being lighted from above and from all sides, the object's scale seems to be absorbed by the atmosphere and the details are lost in the greater need of powerful silhouette and solidity of design. The larger the work the more essential it is to model it simply and always with an eye to meeting the challenge of "reducing" atmosphere.

All experiments and tryouts of arrangement and pose of the subject should be worked out in a small model before the enlarged statue is begun, for this not only permits of greater freedom and ease in the actual work itself, but enables the sculptor to be certain of his results before the enlarged figure is started. It is easy to understand what difficulties would be encountered if serious alterations or shifting of pose had to be made in large-scale arma-tures and heavy clay figures. It is also easier for the eye to grasp the effect of the whole when seen in small size, and for the sculptor to change the design and silhouette of the composition in the small model.

One should be familiar with the various styles of architecture, both of the past centuries and the modern tendencies of one's own day. One should study, in close co-operation with the architect, the type of building on which the reliefs or figures are to be placed, so that the style of the decora-tion will harmonize with the whole effect and be worked out in correct feeling and proportion to the area which surrounds the sculptural design.

If the student would read classic mythology and the fairy tales of different lands, he would find a never-ending well of suggestive ideas. His imagina-tion would be stimulated, and incidentally he would be mentally better equipped with an appreciation of folklore and international culture.

During the past summer I found, near Paris, a decoration in bas-relief by Maurice Saulo on a new primary school. The children were so interested by his clever interpretations of their favorite fairy tales that they would gather in groups and try to identify the subjects. The manner in which he treated the long, narrow strips of his design fitted perfectly into the general architectural scheme of the modern building.

The subject of scale is such an important and yet illusive one! I have heard it well defined by the mural painter, Hildreth Meière: "Scale is like salt. If there is not enough, you miss it; if there is too much, it is disagreeable; if it is just right, you are unconscious of it." When the proportions click, all is well.

Most people, I think, are under the erroneous impression that where sculp-ture is made for decorative purposes on a building, or merely enlarged to monumental scale, the problems for the artist cease when the one-half or one-third models are turned over to the carvers or enlarging craftsmen.

In many cases this is unfortunately true, but if the artist carries through his responsibility, he will know that a heroic figure is not merely a small figure enlarged to heroic proportions. The effect of this procedure is seen in many of our public monuments. They are merely statuettes "blown up," as we call it, to a great size. They therefore lack just those essential qualities that must be felt in heroic work if it is to stand the challenge of endurance and intelligent criticism. When we look at photographs of the great epochs of art, the Egyptian carvings, for example, never give us the impression of small figures enlarged. Their proportions and treatment all give an effect of monumental and inevitable bigness.

The very experience of seeing our own work enlarged to a great scale is a valuable lesson. We realize that certain details must be suppressed; they no longer count. Lines of composition must be strengthened and simplified. The surface texture of the modeling must be so treated that it too assumes the correct value and contributes to the general effect of scale. Delicate folds and details fade away and are eaten up by the size of their new surroundings.

And so the work of the artist is continued to the end. Until the idea is completed in stone or bronze in its final size, he cannot feel at ease. It is all a great gamble of wits and patience, and if in the end the sculptor can feel anything but the desire to do better the next time, he is indeed a lucky individual and a rara avis—or no good!

Might I suggest how architects could help sculptors who enter competitions or work on projects which should conform to architectural settings and scale.

Architects could make scale models of the façade or wall to be decorated, and competitors could try out their sketches in this model to help them to obtain the correct scale. They could try photographs of their models reduced to the correct scale if sketches could not be set in place.

There should be renderings of the building and elevation of the façade, showing the position of the panel over doorways and surrounding windows or walls.

If the competitive panels are exhibited publicly, these should be shown in relation to the scale model to instruct and interest the public; otherwise everyone is lost in a maze, not knowing how to judge the relation of the panels to the setting, existing conditions of light, etc.

An enlarged photograph of the building showing the accepted panel, photographed to scale and colored as the model is colored, would be instructive also. Lighting effects by day and night could readily be indicated on this.

The suitability of the subject matter to its ultimate purpose should be emphasized and the most significant points clearly set forth:

1. Size and scale of figures and decorations.
2. Obvious interest of subject matter as expressing the title of the work in relation to the setting and purpose of the building.
3. Color and material suitable for the special problem.
4. Cost limitations.
5. From where seen and under what lighting conditions.

169. "Justice of Trajan," by R. Romanelli, New Palace of Justice, Milan.

170. "The Dance," by Jean Baptiste Carpeaux,
on the Façade of the Opera House, Paris.

171. Figure for Polish Monument,
by Antoine Bourdelle, Place de l'Alma,
Paris.

172. "La Marseillaise," by François Rude, on the Arc de Triomphe, Paris.

173. *Mausoleum at Cavtat,
Dalmatia, by Ivan Meštrović.*

174. *"Angel of the Soul," by
Ivan Meštrović, One of the Figures
Carved on the Interior Walls of
the Mausoleum.*

175. Bas-relief Representing French Equatorial Africa, by Alfred Auguste Janniot, Colonial Museum, Paris.

176. Maurice Saulo Working on His Bas-relief Illustrating French Fairy Tales, on Modern School Building Near Paris. This Shows How the Stone Is Pointed Up Directly in Place from Plaster Model on the Left.

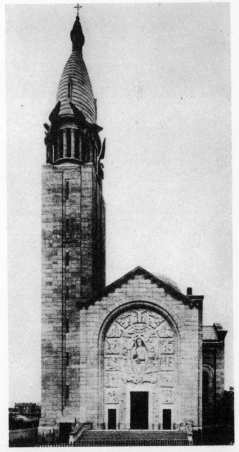

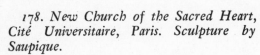

178. New Church of the Sacred Heart, Cité Universitaire, Paris. Sculpture by Saupique.

180. *"Prospero and Ariel," by Eric Gill, Unfinished Soft Stone Model. Group Over Entrance Doorway, Exterior of B.B.C. Building, London (INSIDE COVER)*

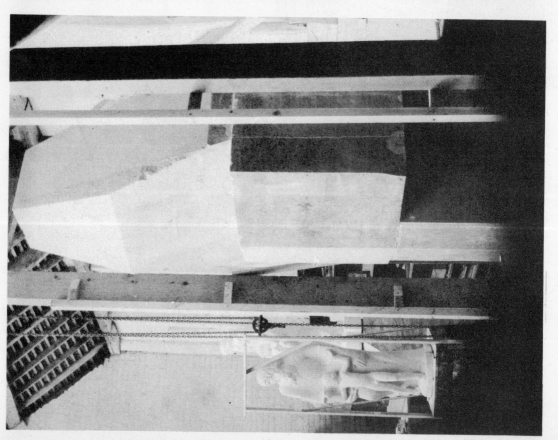

179. *"Prospero and Ariel," by Eric Gill. Blocks of Stone in Workshop Before Beginning of Carving.* (HOWARD COSTER)

181. Artillery Monument by Charles S. Jagger, Hyde Park, London.

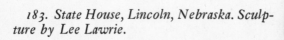

182. *Reliefs by Bainbridge Copnall, Neville House, London.* (JOHN MALTBY)

183. *State House, Lincoln, Nebraska. Sculpture by Lee Lawrie.*

XII. Reliefs and Medals

RELIEFS

THE most essential thing in a relief is the drawing of the design. Before laying on the different levels of the modeled composition, the sculptor generally makes numerous careful studies in charcoal or pencil so that the actual drawing will serve as a preliminary model from which he can proceed with safety to the problem of modeling.

He prepares a flat board, reinforced at the back with strong crossbars or battens that will prevent warping and assure him of a flat, even surface on which to lay his background. He then sees that the corners are square and the boards well shellacked to prevent absorption of moisture. He next fastens two strips of wood to the two sides, projecting to the top level which he wishes to establish for his background. He covers the entire surface with firm clay. When the clay or plasteline has been firmly pressed all over the surface (thicker all over than the projecting edge of the two side strips), he can drive in flat-headed zinc nails to about half the depth of the final background surface. If the relief is a large one, he must tack strips of laths on the boards about four to six inches apart before putting on the clay, and shellac these. If the relief is to be high, he will suspend butterflies on short wires and nail these securely into the wood where he intends to lay on additional depths of his material. When the clay is all pounded on in place, he can draw a strong wire down over the surface, pressing the two ends over the wood strip edges as he draws it down. This will carve off all surplus clay and leave a smooth surface. Another way of doing it is to draw the straight edge of a board over the surface, pressing it down steadily along the side strips. On this he builds up the figures and design of his relief from his drawing; or if he wishes to square off the drawing and enlarge it to the full size, he can then lay it on the smooth clay surface and, following the outlines with a wooden tool, transfer the design to the clay by even pressure. After this he can remove the desired depth of the background with a flat-ended wire tool, and his design will be ready for modeling. It is well to keep a definite outline edge always in relief, so that the design will not fade out into the background. The idea that the relief is a decoration of flat spaces and should appear as an integral part of the wall must be kept in mind, for this will warn the sculptor not to make too deep undercuts or dark accents.

As in other forms of sculpture, the final permanent material in which a work is to be made will impose its own limitations on the sculptor's manner of interpretation. A subject destined for bronze is not modeled in the same manner as one to be carved in marble. The main pattern of the composition should be kept as simple as possible, when it is to be carved in stone, and surface details should be carefully subordinated to the more important features of the design and dignity of the composition if it is to be carried out in heroic proportion. For, as I have emphasized before, every branch of sculpture demands a different treatment, depending on the scale and ultimate setting of each piece of work. It is not possible to judge the final effect accurately on a small model, no matter how carefully it is prepared, and it should be the duty and privilege of every sculptor to restudy and work over the enlarged model, adding whatever he feels may enhance its beauty or simplify its design in the monumental final size. To leave this part of the work to the mercy of an enlarging machine, even when guided by the hand of the finest craftsman, is to side-step one of the most crucial phases of his responsibility to his art.

There is an alarming influence today that has the objective of classifying the creative artist in the same category as the organized craftsmen, and which tries to persuade the sculptor, when he has completed a quarter-size model, to turn this over to an enlarging concern and agree to step aside. If the creator of a work of art is willing to leave a single stone unturned that might enable him to improve upon his original model, if he sees that certain changes would simplify and enhance the significance of his work and fails to give of his best up to the very last moment, he is unworthy to be called an artist. Let the public be warned of this, for such a lowering of the standards of art would soon be a national menace that would not only result in the decadence of quality in art, but its evil effects would be felt in innumerable directions.

185. *Carved Ivory Tusk from Benin, Africa, Louis Carré Collection, Paris.*

184. *Chinese Bronze Libation Cup,* 1122-255 B.C., *Chou Dynasty, Freer Gallery of Art, Washington, D. C.*

186. Stone Relief of Animals in Roman Forum. (ANDERSON)

187. "Unknown Warrior," by Desiderio da Settignano, Italian Renaissance.
(METROPOLITAN MUSEUM)

188. *Decorative Vase by John Gregory, American Sculptor.*
(DE WITT WARD)

189. *Eidsvoll Commemorative Column in Granite (Not Yet Finished) by Professor Vilhelm Robert Rasmussen, Norwegian Sculptor.*

190. Sketch for Bas-relief by René Chambellan.

MODEL 26

191. Plaster Model of Bas-relief by René Chambellan, Showing Finished Version

(DREYER)

192. Process of Casting Large Relief, Gelatine Molds.

193. International Dance Fountain, by Malvina Hoffman. These Seven Figures from Different Countries Are Framed in the Decorative Design of Their Various Local Flora, Trees, Cactus Plants, and the Symbols Representing the Countries of Their Origin. The Cylindrical Form of a Perforated Bas-relief Is Seen in Silhouette Against a Colored Inner Cylinder of Glass. This Inner Cylinder Is Flooded by Indirect Lighting so That at Night the White Figures Are Seen Against a Glowing Green Glass Background. The Foundation of the Fountain Is Faced With Green Glass Bricks, and the Encircling Pool, 60 Feet in Diameter, Reflects the Design of Sculptured Figures in Its Still Surface. A Wide Walk Around the Pool Is Edged with a Dark Green Trimmed Hedge of Fir Trees. This Hedge Begins at the Pool at the Height of Three Feet, and Grows Higher and Higher as It Spirals Around the Garden, Until It Reaches the Height of 16 Feet.

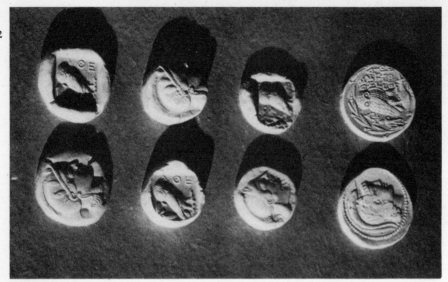

194. *Ancient Greek Coins, Collection of M. H.*
(NUMISMATIC MUSEUM, ATHENS)

MEDALS

The art of carving a design into a hard stone or engraving it onto the surface of a gem is known as "intaglio," whereas if the design is carved in relief on the stone it is called "cameo." These two arts were highly developed by the Greeks and Romans and carried on brilliantly during the Italian Renaissance. The sculptor modeled his original in wax, and then the actual carving of the stone was done by very hard, metallic tools turned swiftly by a sort of lathe and guided by the artist's hand.

In the olden days, when coins did not have to be piled up so high in mints or banks and therefore did not demand the flatness of relief of modern money, there was a greater liberty of design and wonderful variety in the style of numismatic modeling.

The old medal masters made their originals the size of the actual medal, and wondrous indeed are the bold, simple forms of their portrait heads and prancing steeds. They were able to reduce a personal portrait into a timeless, generic type. All unnecessary details were eliminated, and the important elements accented with authority and style.

The sculptor must work his design in constantly changing lights, so that the relief reads convincingly. His forms must be laid on in careful relation to each other, and the feeling of the whole mass must be always in his mind. Too strong an accent on any one part can destroy the entire composition.

In medal designing the artist is often called upon to suggest appropriate symbolism or floral motifs, such as laurel or palm leaves, vestal virgins, serpents, sacrificial altars, armor, or modern skyscrapers. Lettering of all types, and careful spacing of these elements, constitutes a liberal education in itself.

It is because of this endless range of subjects and inevitable need of information that throughout this book I have stressed the point that the sculptor should read and study when he is not actually working in the studio. Art is not an eight-hour day but rather a twelve- to fourteen-hour day with no time clocks or overseers either to drive us ahead or to lock us out of our own workshops. When the mind feels itself in a receptive, hungry mood it should be trained to absorb and remember long periods of reading.

Making careful notes and sketches while studying a new subject helps to retain the new impressions and store them in the brain, where they soak in and gradually form a subconscious foundation of intelligence and humility; for the more one learns, the more one realizes how small is the actual knowledge of the average mind, and how urgent is the need for each one of us to develop his own and inner self.

Today, sculptors generally model their design about four times again as large as the medal will be when finished. The design can be modeled in low or high relief and a plaster mold made. On this reverse negative the artist can retouch and perfect his design by working directly on the plaster. From this stage he can press in another mold of wax or plasteline and obtain the positive impression. While working, it is useful to squeeze the wax often against the negative mold, thereby verifying just what the effect will be in the positive before actually making the final plaster cast.

The next step is to procure from these models a metal mold, and the most successful method of doing this is by the galvano process. The plaster models are waxed and a coat of either graphite or bronze powder is applied on the surface. A copper wire is arranged around the plaster model. On the back of the model is applied a nonconductive preparation, leaving only the surface where the metal is desired exposed to copper anodes.

Anodes (sheets of copper) are hung in a tank filled with an acid solution. A copper bar is set across the tank, and this bar is charged with a certain voltage of electric current from a positive terminal. The models (or cathodes) are now immersed in the solution and are hung about eight inches below the surface of the acid bath on another metal bar attached to the negative terminal. Owing to the proper current, a thin layer of copper is deposited on the surface of the (cathode) model; this is drawn from the copper anodes.*

By leaving these models in the tank for twenty-four to sixty hours, a proper thickness of copper is deposited on the plaster. We thus get a perfect copper mold, assuring a faithful replica of the model to the most minute detail. These copper molds are now ready for the die-cutting machine.

This machine has a flat bed on top, upon which are mounted three chariots. Two of these chariots, A and B, are stationary. The center chariot is free to be moved up or down according to the size of reduction or die that is required. The proportional reduction from the size of the mold to the size of the die is arrived at by a mathematical formula.

On the bed of the die-cutting machine is a scale rule divided into millimeters, and the central movable chariot can be placed on the proper point where the die of a certain dimension is required. The head chariot A is stationary, as I have said above. On this chariot is fastened a plateau, upon which the mold is attached.

To the moving chariot C is applied a chuck. This chuck holds the steel

* See page 307 for electrodeposition.

195. Die-cutting Machine. (MEDALLIC ART CO.)

196. Copper Mold on Right Being Reproduced in Smaller Scale on Soft Steel on Left. (MEDALLIC ART CO.)

197. Annealing Medals. (MEDALLIC ART CO.)

198. Press for Stamping Out Final Medals, Capacity 1000 Tons.

(MEDALLIC ART CO.)

upon which the die is to be cut. The fixed chariot B on the other end has a steel bar that works on a pivot. This steel bar is brought up to the center of the mold by means of a rotating screw which acts as a lever to raise the bar. Then a tracer is applied to this bar and centered exactly on the mold.

Facing the steel that is held in the chuck is a rotating drill. Great care has to be exercised in setting the drill in correct proportion to the tracer. This must conform, in ratio, as the size of the mold is to the die which is to be cut. Both the plateau that holds the mold and the chuck that holds the steel rotate together, clockwise, by means of a gear. When the machine is started, the bar holding the tracer and revolving drill very slowly, imperceptibly so, moves downwards, which causes the tracer, as well as the drill, to operate on a spiral. A spring pulls the bar towards the surface of the steel and the mold.

A coat of vaseline has been applied to the mold, and a flow of oil runs on the drill so as not to overheat it, for this would cause it to break. It is well to mention here that the steel from which the die is being cut is soft. It is necessary to repeat this cutting operation two or three times.

The first operation is a rough cutting; the second is more accurate than the first, and the finished operation simply smooths over the steel. The die is now completed. It is removed from the chuck, and hardened and tempered. This is done by heating the steel to a certain degree and then immersing it in cold water. The die is now ready for stamping medals, and this is done as follows.

A flat piece of bronze, silver, or gold is cut out to the size of the die, and the die is then placed on a press. This press operates with a capacity from low pressure of a few pounds to a high pressure of one thousand tons. To give you an idea of what is required on a set of dies about three inches in diameter, the pressure needed to bring out a fair relief would be from four to seven hundred tons.

The metal requires several operations of stamping to bring it to the full relief that exists in the die. Between each stamping it is necessary to anneal the metal so as to resoften it to its original state.

When the metal is fully stamped, the surplus metal that forms on the edges from the pressure of the press is turned off on a lathe. We now have a complete medal. This medal is cleaned in acid, sandblasted to give it a mat finish, and then treated with a sulphur solution.

A limitless variety of tones and coloring may be obtained by patining bronze medals with acids, just as is done to the other forms of bronze sculpture in the round.

XIII. *Animals*

THE sculptor should not limit his studies to the vagaries and appearances of only the human race; he should visit the menageries and botanical gardens and observe the forms and movements of animals, plants, and trees, both wild and domestic. By making a great number of careful drawings of animals he can familiarize himself with their most striking characteristics, both in action and repose, and study the flora and fauna of their native habitats. The study of the skeleton and muscular construction of the animal is an essential preliminary. The manner in which the head and legs move and are held in place is the next step in the understanding of their anatomy.

In 1927 I went to Zagreb to study horses in sculpture, under the direction of Ivan Meštrović. Just outside the city there was a horse-breeding farm, and there I could examine and draw splendid examples of Arab stallions, Irish hunters, and English hackneys, all of which were being bred and trained for the cavalry regiments of Yugoslavia. After making many drawings and a complete model about two feet high of one of the stallions, I modeled a life-sized head and made studies of the horse's legs in standing and action poses. Meštrović then advised me to model very exactly the skull of a horse and make a copy of the heroic marble head by Phidias which we know so well in the Elgin Marble Room of the British Museum. After this, I made two reliefs representing horsemen in different attitudes.

Realizing quite well that all these items of my personal experience are of no importance to others except as suggestions to students who may not know quite how to proceed, I submit them with modesty; for no one realizes until he has been in the harness a long time how elastic are all rules and regulations to the born artist, who will find means of acquiring knowledge by the same natural laws that guide an animal in a jungle. Self-preservation will give him the cue and the courage to go ahead.

199. *Tiger, Chinese Sculpture in Bronze, Chou Dynasty or Earlier, Decoration Cast in Low Relief, Freer Gallery of Art, Washington.*

200. *Prancing Pig, Pompeian Bronze, National Museum, Naples.* (ALINARI)

201. *Faun, Antique Bronze, National Museum, Naples.*

(ALINARI)

Nearly all of us have dogs, cats, or birds in our homes, and if we are not lucky enough to own a horse, we can generally interest some friend who does own one to lend him to us as a model for a few hours from time to time. A pure-blooded Siamese cat can teach us a lot about Egyptian sculpture and our fellow man and the dignity of animal behavior.

In Paris, after returning from Zagreb, I found a studio in an *impasse* near the horse markets, and here I was able to hire different types of horses as models for continuing my studies. By hitching the horse to a post outside the big studio door, I was able to model and make friends with the animal, so that we soon understood each other; my neighbors would smile at the scene when, after eating some sugar or a handful of oats, the horse would lift his front leg and place his hoof on a box and stay in this pose as patiently as if he were standing on his four legs. This enabled me to study the knee in action and gradually understand the construction of his bodily forms and proportions.

In many equestrian statues, anatomical accents and details detract from the simple and powerful forms in the bodies of the animals. The conformation of a lion needs little else than the true relation of the main masses and planes to express his dignified omnipotence. The panther has inspired some splendid sculptural representations in black marble or stone.

Encourage children not only to play with animals, but teach them how to observe and understand them. If they do this they will not carelessly tease them or be afraid of them when they grow up. Rather will they take pride in the intelligent care and training of their animal friends, and if they have to model or paint them they will feel in sympathy with them.

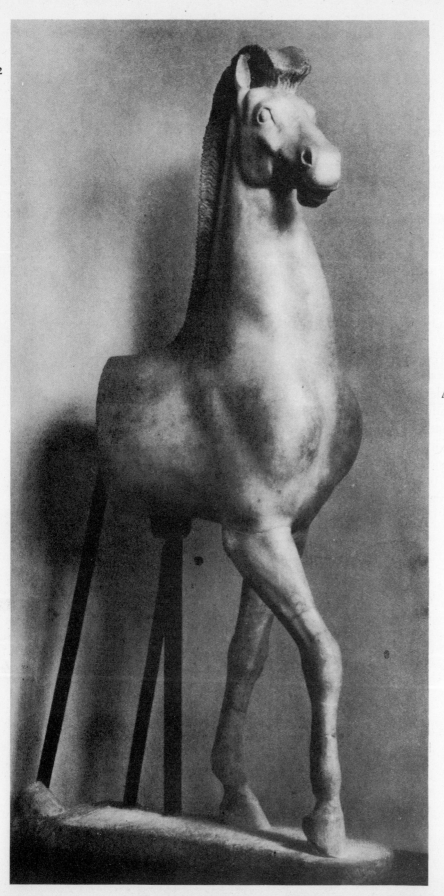

202. Greek Horse,
Marble, About 500 B.C.

203. *Top of a Mask Representing Crouching Antelope, Wood Carving, French Sudan, Louis Carré Collection, Paris.*

204. *Native Horn Carving of Bird, from the Island of Madagascar.*

205. Percheron Mare and Foal by Herbert Haseltine, Bardiglio Marble.

206. Eagle by Matéo Hernandez, Black Marble.

207. Prancing Foal by Renée Sintenis, German Sculptor.

208. Zebra by Kurt Schwerdtfeger.

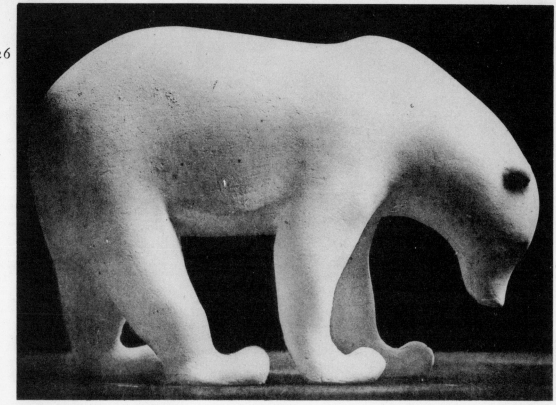

209. Polar Bear by François Pompon, Paris.

210. Pigeon by Joel and Jan Martel, Paris. (CHARLES MOREAU)

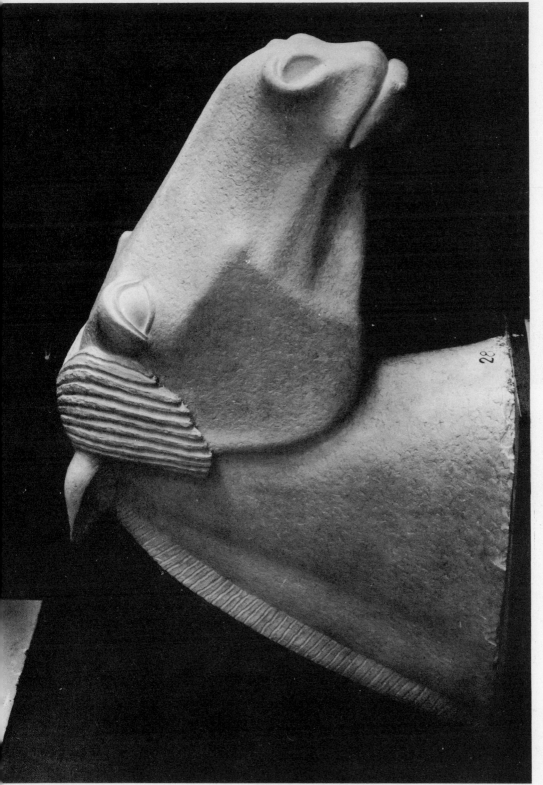

*211. Detail of Equestrian Monument by Anne Grimdalen, Norwegian Sculptor,
Winner of Oslo City Hall Competition, 1938.*

212. Katharine Lane Modeling *Rhinoceros* for the *Biological Laboratory, Harvard University.*

213. Marshall Fredericks, *American Sculptor, Cranbrook, Michigan.*

XIV. Enlarging and Reducing

ENLARGING BY A WOODEN FRAME

Making Two Rectangular Frames for Enlargement of a Model (to Four Times the Size, for Example)

1. *Small Model Frame* A

Prepare four strips of wood ½″ thick and ¾″ wide for top. Nail them together to form a rectangle with square 90° corners, the two short ones inside the ends of the two long ones. Each strip should be slightly longer than the maximum measurement on the model. Divide and mark the strips into inches, left to right, ¼″ and ⅛″, and mark a central point. Four uprights exactly the same length must be nailed to the four inner corners of the top of the frame and set over the four corners of the wooden base, perfectly vertical, so the frame will be exactly horizontal. Verify all these points; a plumb line and level must be used.

2. *Enlarged-size Frame* B

Make this exactly the same way, but four times larger in every sense. The wood must be heavier and reinforced to keep its exact right-angle corners. Mark off in inches and fractions, as before. B must be set over the large-size armature to clear the top of figure, and rest on the base.

3. For taking points prepare two strips of smooth wood of the entire height of small frame, with crosspiece at the top end as a projection on which they hang. Measure off inches on entire length of these on both sides. Make two other height sticks four times longer for large frame (one for

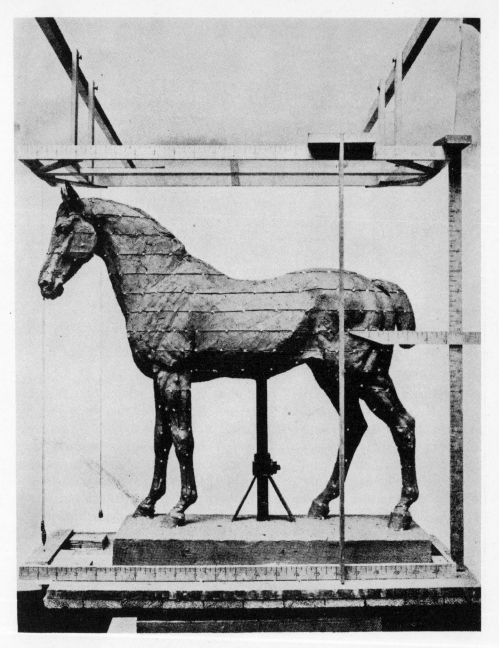

214. Enlarging by Wooden Frame. (FROM "MODELLING," VOL. III, BY E. LANTERI)

Upper Frame May Be Supported on Four Uprights as Described in Text.

front and one for side of frame). Cut two straight measuring sticks ½″ thick, 1″ wide, for finding depth points, one four times the length of the other. Measure off both sides in inches. When the frames are assembled they must fit over the figures with even projection all around. A center should be established by drawing two lines between four diagonal corners. Where they intersect will be the center.

Pointing Up

1. Draw horizontal lines on model about 1″ apart. Mark dots every 1½″ on these lines. (Use a level.)

2. On small model take height of first line on height measure stick (at 4″, for example). Place height measure stick on large frame (at 16″). Place measuring stick at right angles toward the model and draw a horizontal line on clay. (Use a level.)

3. The same procedure for all other lines.

4. For speed, two people should work together; one takes depth and distance points on model, calling measures to the other, who takes them on the large model.

5. To get the depth of the point, measure the distance from point of measuring stick on model to the inner edge of height measure which hangs on the frame. Four times this will be the point on large size.

6. To get the lateral distance of a point, place point of measure stick on the point of the model, and note the distance from the tip to the inner edge of the second height measure which hangs on the side of the frame, and mark point four times this distance on enlarged model.

This whole process may be reversed when a model is to be reduced instead of enlarged.

Since the perfection of pointing machines has been developed, this wooden frame process is not often used. The machine performs its task more rapidly, and therefore saves time and expense.

In the case of a relief, a similar frame may be set over the front and the surface measured off in the same manner. For depths the height stick may be perforated with a slot, and a pointer (marked with a scale), with setscrew, may be pushed through this to the proper distance and the setscrew placed at four times longer distance from the point.

TO ENLARGE A RELIEF
(*To Twice the Size*)

To enlarge a figure in the center flanked by decorations on each side, square off the small model by setting nails in a frame above and below and on each end of the panel. The size and number of squares may be arbitrary, provided they are identical over the entire area (see diagram I). On the enlargement divide the area into the same number of divisions as on the model, each division to be twice the distance apart in every sense.

HOW TO CHANGE PROPORTIONS IN SQUARING OFF AN ENLARGEMENT (*To Twice the Size*)

The sculptor decides that in his model the figure appears too cramped laterally, and decides to increase the length of the *figure only* and keep the end panels in the same proportion. The original model is squared off as described above. The limiting lines on the original figure in the model are drawn in, A′A′, B′B′ (see diagram I). Draw limiting lines AA-BB which indicate the distance to which the figure is to be lengthened, XX. The enlarged panel is prepared in the same way as described above. There will be the same number of divisions in height over the entire panel, twice the distance apart (the end panels, for instance, no change in proportion being desired, are marked off vertically with corresponding divisions twice the distance apart). The central panel AA-BB now includes the additional areas XX. This must now be divided into the *identical* number of divisions as the area A′A′, B′B′ in the small model, starting from the center in both cases. It will be found that the areas in the enlargement in this case will be wider than they are high, because each square now includes its portion of the areas XX required for the length of the figure (see diagram II).

This principle can, of course, be applied to expanding vertically as well as reducing width and height as required.

The advantage of having the projecting frame with nails and of squaring off by strings on a very large relief is that one may pull them to one side easily or even temporarily unlace a section while attaching the necessary armature to the background and drawing in the larger design. Such a problem was recently met by René Chambellan, sculptor, and ingeniously solved in this way.

For depth points a ruler may be held against the string at right angles to the surface of the small model. Twice this distance will give correct depth of point on large model (for twice the size enlargement).

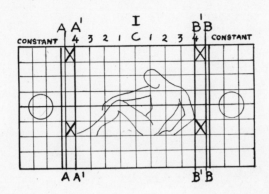

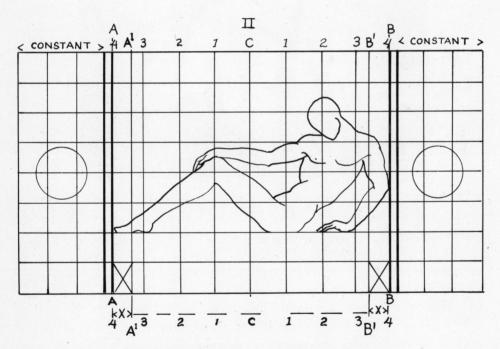

215. *Diagram Illustrating Method of Enlarging.*

TO ENLARGE BY THREE-CALIPER AND POST
METHOD

To enlarge a relief, for example one and a half times, set four corner points on model 1-2-3-4. Take one and a half times distance between each and transfer to model to be enlarged. Check with calipers. Set posts on surface of model at convenient spots for taking depth points from their top —a long flat-headed nail set in plaster (with pin point drilled in center of head). These posts must be set near enough to one another to act as the

216. Enlarging by 3-Caliper and Post System.

centers of two overlapping circular areas. The radius of each must not exceed the height of the post. This will give an angle of 45° at the tip, inside of which you may take accurate measures for depth. For greater area raise height of posts until entire surface of relief is covered by their radii, or place an additional short post for the small uncovered area.

Proceed as follows. To take point X place one leg of caliper 1 on corner point 1 on small model, and other leg on point X. Measure its distance on a scale * and stretch it to one and a half times this length. Take caliper 2 from point 2 (small model) to X, and stretch it one and a half times this distance.

* See page 172.

For depth put one leg of caliper Y on tip of post Y (small model) and other leg to point X. Stretch it to one and a half times this distance.

Now you have your three calipers set for establishing point X on enlargement. Begin at point 1 on large model with one leg of caliper 1; describe arc on surface. Take caliper 2—one leg on point 2 of large model; describe arc intersecting arc made by number 1.

Take caliper Y, one leg on tip of post Y, and when arc described by this shorter caliper intersects the spot where the first two arcs intersected, your depth point will be exactly determined.

Always proceed in this sequence—take long points before short one so they will all work toward one another; when an area is pointed accurately, move on and follow same method on post 2, and so on until enlarged model is completed.

This three-caliper method with posts can also be used when carving figures in the round.

PANTOGRAPH, AN INSTRUMENT FOR ENLARGING OR REDUCING DRAWINGS

I shall begin by describing proportional dividers.

Proportional dividers, or compasses, are used to enlarge or reduce. The pivot of the dividers is held in a slide in the longitudinal slots of its two legs, and is secured by a setscrew. The dimensions are measured by one pair of points and transferred with the other pair; the enlargement or reduc-

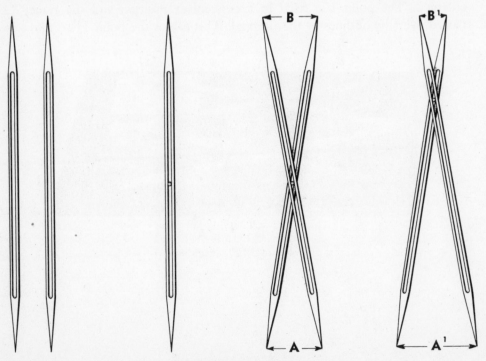

217. Proportional Dividers.

tion will be in proportion to the relative distances of the points from the pivot. A scale is marked on the legs to determine the proportion.

Reduced to the simplest formula, take two straight, parallel lines ending in points. Superimpose one upon the other. Fasten these in the center with a setscrew, which will be held in a sliding plate, which in turn may be pushed along the slot in the legs. It will be readily seen that if the setscrew is in the center, the distance between both end points A and B will be equal.

If setscrew is moved along towards the end B_1, the distance between these two points decreases, and the distance between A_1 points increases in proportion. If B_1 measures one-third the distance of A_1, no matter how far apart you open the points, one pair (A_1) will always give you three times the other pair (B_1), until you change the position of the setscrew.

The invention of the pantograph is ascribed to Christoph Scheiner, a Jesuit, in 1603. It has since undergone various modifications and improvements.

The pantograph consists of four strips of wood, two of which, A and B, are jointed at C, and the other two, D and E, are jointed over H. Each strip is perforated with a series of numbered holes, and D and E are provided with thumb screws F by which they may be connected to A and B at any of the holes of the series. G is a tracer; H, a pencil or pricker; and I, a screw attached to the drawing board to hold the instrument in position.

For use, the strips D and E are secured to the others by inserting the thumb screws through the holes marked with the numbers (as ¾, ½, ⅓, ¼, etc.) corresponding with the scale to which the drawing is to be reduced or enlarged. The point I is fixed in a convenient position and the tracer G passed over the outlines of the original. This causes the point H to move in

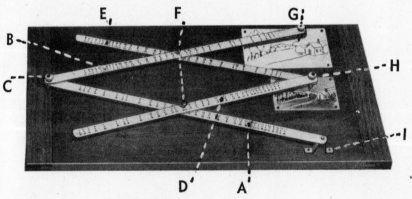

218. Pantograph. (BRUNING CO.)

a direction parallel to that of the tracer, the extent of its motion being governed by the adjustment above described.*

If a pencil point is used it draws a design or figure similar to the original but differing from it in size. In straight-line drawings it is more usual to use a plain needle point, pricking a sufficient number of points into the paper to serve as a guide to the draftsman, who afterwards connects them by lines.

The point G on this diagram of the pantograph may be considered as the tracer point B on the French-type "Colas" machine on a following page, and H as the cutter point. I would represent the universal joint. Line A would be 9 (French), while D is 7 (French), and E is 8 (French); the last two are the parallel links.

Let us hope that it will be easier to understand the complicated mechanism of the machines which follow, now that the pantograph has been explained.

* This principle is easily understood by observing a "lazy tongs." Here each set of connecting links has the same movement as the set before it, but the combined movements of all the sets of links amount to the movement of any one set multiplied by the number of sets.

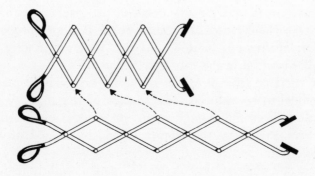

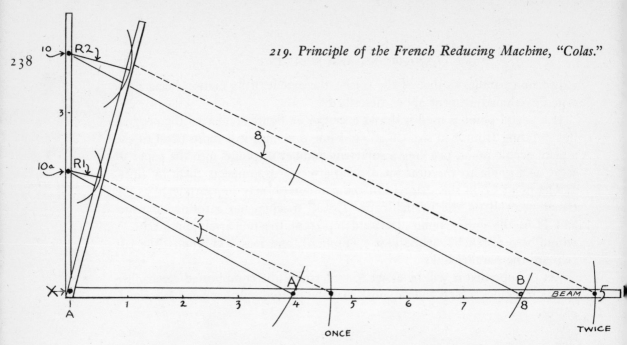

The Radius at R1 is One-half the Length of the Radius at R2. Any Arc Described at R2 Will Be Twice as Long as the Arc Described by the Same Movement at R1. If These Movements Are Transmitted by Suitable Linkage (as by Bars C and D) to Sliders on the Horizontal Beam E, the Slider B Connected With R2 Will Move Twice the Distance Along the Beam E That Will Be Traversed by the Slider A Connected With R1. (See Diagram on Page 240 for Full Explanation.)

REDUCING SCULPTURE BY PANTOGRAPH MACHINE (FRENCH TYPE)

In This Case to One-half Size

1. It is important to verify every detail of the machine with a spirit level, and see that tracer and cutter are placed in the positions proper to give the required enlargement or reduction, and that they are exactly opposite the guiding needles inserted in the carriages A and B.

2. On the carriage table B at the right, fix firmly with plaster and jute the plaster model to be reduced. The surface of this must be *very hard* or the point will sink in and scratch it, giving inaccuracies in the reduction. The plaster cast should be thoroughly dried and heated in an oven, and stearined while hot.

3. Prepare a roll of sheet zinc or tin ¹⁄₃₂″ gauge, slightly higher and wider than the size of the desired reduced model and so rolled that the edges are considerably overlapped. This should be secured by binding a wire around it.

4. Set second carriage table, which is to bear the reduction, on the floor. Fasten the cylinder to this with strong plaster ring, and close the overlap crack with same, inside and out, for the entire height, to prevent liquid

220. Colas Machine Set at One-half Reduction.

plaster leaking out. When the plaster seams are firmly set, place the carriage table in its geared holder and mark on the tin cylinder the height to which the plaster must be poured. This is done by raising the beam so that the pointer is, say, an inch above the top of the work to be reduced, and marking with a pencil the height of the cutting tool.

5. Now prepare the plaster for pouring by stirring with the hand gently as it is sifted into the water and eliminating all lumps. The exact consistency of the plaster is a matter to be determined only by trial and error. If it is too thin, the reduction will break easily; if too hard, it will be difficult to work. Try at all times to avoid making bubbles.

6. When ready to pour, remove the carriage table from the machine and, having placed it on a bench, pour the plaster gently into the cylinder up to the mark made. By feeling the top it is easy to determine when the plaster is sufficiently set to take off its tin wrapper, which is done by unwinding the wire, chipping away the plaster seals with great care, and then lifting the carriage table into and locking it in its holder (21) by the setscrews.

7. Be extremely careful, when starting to shave off the fresh plaster surface with the sharp reducing pointer, not to knock or push against the solid, fresh cylinder of plaster; otherwise it may be detached from its carriage base and all the work will have to be done over.

8. Begin at the top and bear gently and evenly downward and outward in roughing out the new plaster. Work steadily and as fast as possible in strokes one-eighth inch apart. For roughing out, the tracer for the model

should carry a pad of felt over its point, held on by a bit of adhesive tape. This added length will save you from cutting away too much on the reduced model until all the forms are safely indicated and the surface ready to be exactly pointed.

9. Every stroke of the tracer, guided steadily over the planes of the large model, must be made at right angles to the planes. Keep turning the guide beam constantly, so that your tracer aims directly over each plane, and revolve the work by turning 23 so that there is a minimum of lateral movement of the cutter and tracer. Too many cuts being taken without turning the work (as often as the planes permit) is one of the most common causes of error in the reduction. The motion of the cutter should always be from left to right when working. A perfect result shows no lines on the surface.

10. Be careful to wipe machine clean whenever you stop working. The wet plaster and finger marks, etc., will cause rust. Every part of the machine should be kept bright and clean and rubbed with oil. A good engineer keeps his machine shining and takes pride in its appearance.

11. The tracer and cutter must, before commencing work, be set to the exact length from the beam to the center of the spider (6) in the universal joint, and the cutter (which is sharpened triangularly) must be set at a slight angle in order to present a cutting edge to the work.

221. Diagram of Colas Machine Set at One-half Reduction. Dotted Lines Show Change of Proportionate Reduction to One-third.

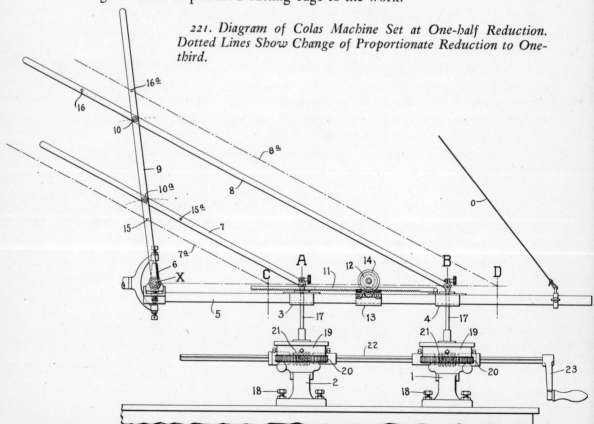

12. The machine is set for a one-half reduction, the cutter being located at "A" and the tracer at "B." These are securely held in sliding brackets 3 and 4 carried on the beam 5, which is supported at one end by the universal joint 6 and at its other extremity by the cord O leading to an overhead pulley and a counterbalance weight which are not shown.

Pivotally connected to the sliding brackets 3 and 4 are the connecting links 7 and 8 respectively, which in turn are pivotally connected to the upwardly extending arm 9 by means of the thumb screws 10 and 10a.

Connected to the top surface of the bracket 4 is the rack bar 11 which is in mesh with one of a train of gears 12 carried by the stationary bracket 13 clamped on the beam 5.

The gears 12 are caused to rotate by means of the hand wheel 14, and any rotary movement given this wheel is transferred to the bracket 4 only, as bracket 3 is not connected to the rack bar 11.

The bracket 3 is moved along the beam 5 by its connecting link 7, the arm 9, and the connecting link 8; it being readily seen that when the bracket 4 is moved toward the right, for example, by the rack bar 11 it will pull upon its connecting link 8, which in turn will pull the arm 9 in a clockwise direction, thereby causing said arm to push the connecting link 7 toward the right-hand side of the machine, sliding the bracket 3 with it in the same direction, but only one-half the distance that bracket 4 moved. This of course is due to the relative proportion between the points BX and AX, to 10X and 10AX (BX : AX : : 10 X : 10AX).

If it should be wished to change the proportion of reduction, for example to one-third:

First, take out the thumb screw 10a and then slide the bracket 3 toward the left until the holes 15 and 15a of the arm 9 and link 7 coincide, and place the thumb screw in position. This will bring the cutter into the position indicated at "C."

Now remove the thumb screw 10 and move the bracket 4 toward the right until the holes 16 and 16a of the arm 9 and link 8 coincide, and replace the thumb screw. This places the tracer in the position as indicated at "D," the links 7 and 8 taking the parallel positions of the dot and dash lines 7a and 8a respectively.

Any ratio of reduction or enlargement may be made by supplying the arm and links with suitably located thumb screw holes as in the well-known pantograph drawing machine.

The carriages 1 and 2, as already mentioned, are for supporting the model and the block of plaster to be cut. To locate their position in relation to the center of the cutter and tracer, it is first necessary to fasten in position the locating spindles 17. When the points of these spindles coincide with the points of the cutter and tracer, as illustrated in Figure 220, at "A" and "B," the carriages are then secured in position on the bed of the machine by means of the setscrews 18.

The carriage tables 19 are rotated by the worm gears 20 and the worms 21, slidably mounted on the shaft 22, which is rotated by the crank 23.

To increase the size of work it is easily seen that if the model to be reproduced were placed in position on carriage 2 and the plaster block to be cut were placed in position on carriage 1, and the cutter and pointer reversed, an increase of two times the size would be obtained.

Different cutter tools are necessary if the enlarged model is to be scraped from a block of plasteline or clay, the most satisfactory being a loop of watch spring bound and then soldered into a steel rod.

222. Cutter Tool for Plasteline Enlargement on French Type of Machine.

ROBERT PAYNE MACHINE

First Used for the Buffalo Pan-American Exhibition of 1901

The arm carrying the pointers is made of a hollow tube of aluminum four inches in diameter. It is supported at one-third and two-thirds of its distance by a hanging bar which is swung on a rope from a pulley at the top, with a counterweight. This two-point support prevents sagging of the long arm and assures accuracy of pointing.

The small model is securely attached above and below to turntables. The large model is attached in the same manner to two other turntables. The two turntables on top are geared together by an endless chain. By this means, whenever the large model is turned, the small one turns exactly the same distance. Both the turntables on which the models are set revolve on a steel track set on the floor.

The two pointers, one proportionately longer than the other, operate laterally in unison, by the connecting bar, and may be raised or lowered on the surfaces of both small and large models, as they are carried on the long, hanging arm of the machine. They shift laterally, but as the points are

(seen from above)

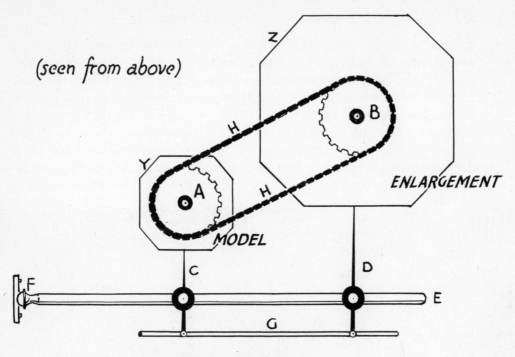

A-B *Sprocket Wheels on Turntables*
C-D *Small & Long Pointers*
E- *Arm-Pivoting from (F) the*
F- *Universal Joint (Secured to Wall)*
G- *Connecting Rod for Shifting Direction of Pointers*
H- *Chain*
Y-Z *Turntables on Iron Beam Set on the Floor*

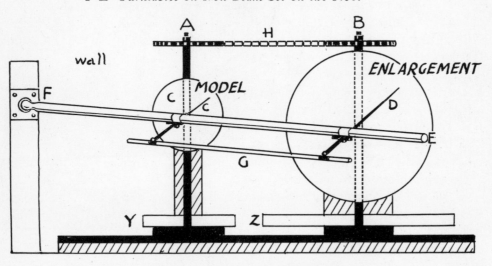

223. Robert Payne Enlarging Machine.

straight, when the model has undercuts the larger model must be turned so that the parts to be pointed may be reached by the tips of both pointers without scratching any of the surfaces or projecting forms. Great care must be taken when setting up this machine to assure accuracy, for if any point is wrong on the small model such an error becomes enlarged in ratio to the increased proportion of the larger model. The latter may be built up in clay on a wooden frame, or directly in plaster on a metal armature. The latter method obviates making a plaster *cast* on a clay enlargement, but also necessitates knowledge of plaster-modeling technique.

224. Studio of René Chambellan, Where the Quarter-size Model of the International Dance Fountain by Malvina Hoffman Was Enlarged Four Times, Total Height 16 Feet. Payne Machine Seen at the Back, Taking Points to Build Up the Supporting Armature on a Wooden Cylinder for the Figure of Dancing Girl of Bali. On Left, "Tom-tom Player of Africa" Prepared and Pointed to Receive Clay Surface. Back of This, "American Indian Dancing"; on the Right, "Cambodian Dancer." (LOUIS DREYER)

225. *Balinese Figure, More Advanced, on the Right. "European Dancer" on the Left, Miss Hoffman Raising Small Model Into the Air by Electric Pulley.*

(BERENICE ABBOTT)

When the small-sized model is completed in clay, it is generally cast into plaster; on the surface of this the craftsman places pencil marks, following the main lines of the larger contours and keeping to the high points all over the figure. Sometimes it is found wise to draw lines down the forms indicating the main planes, and then across all these forms at the desired distance. The points of intersection of these lines indicate where points should be taken.

On a metal bar are set two holders for curved metal points B and C. This bar is attached to point A. The holders are turned by a geared wheel at D, working the rod. D is turned by the left hand. These point holders may be adjusted on the bar to any proportion needed, either to enlarge or to reduce a model. In the former case the short point touches the surface of the plaster model, while the long point is set to register twice or four times (or more) the size of the smaller one. If curved needles are used, the curve of the long one is proportionately longer than that of the shorter needle.

When making heroic-sized enlargements, it is better if one person controls the small point so that it does not scrape or injure the surface of the plaster when taking a point, while another holds the large point and takes the necessary measurements to which the framework and armature must be built. Of course additional space must be allowed for the clay by leaving projecting nails or points attached to the basic wooden armature. The nails may be driven in until their heads touch the point of the long curved pointer. The exact heights of these nail heads determine the final surface.

If the enlargement is to be in plasteline, as each measurement is taken on the small model the point is set in the enlarged plasteline model by pushing a little match or half a toothpick into the surface of the plasteline until its projecting end touches the long pointer.

The plasteline should be built up freely in small lumps pressed around the points firmly so they will not shift their positions. Build up the surface from within, carefully, so as to avoid having to take off excess plasteline.

On this pointed surface the sculptor works and finishes the enlarged subject with his own technique. Some sculptors push the points in as they finish the surface. Others prefer to have all the points removed (plucked out) as soon as the enlargement is completed. This leaves the artist entirely free to make whatever changes he may feel are necessary.

It is important that the long arm of the machine be made of rigid metal, and the points must be verified occasionally to avoid distortions or errors caused by too much sag or play in the apparatus.

Generally speaking, for a heroic figure the most convenient method is to construct the main armature in three- by two-inch pine posts and onto this skeleton to nail crosspieces of lathing, leaving space enough between each lath to squeeze the clay so it will not shift when weight is added to it. The wood should be well shellacked.

In building up very large reliefs on wooden frames, it is sometimes useful to point the main outline of the design, drawing this on the wooden background; to hold the weight of clay from shifting, just inside this outline drive in long spikes and fasten wire mesh (on edge) to these. Reinforce this with burlap dipped in plaster. It is flexible and light to handle and easier to remove afterwards than a complicated wooden reinforcement.

There are many other pointing machines in use today, some with pneumatic drill attachments or electric motors to turn and shift the carriages, but the basic principles show little variation.

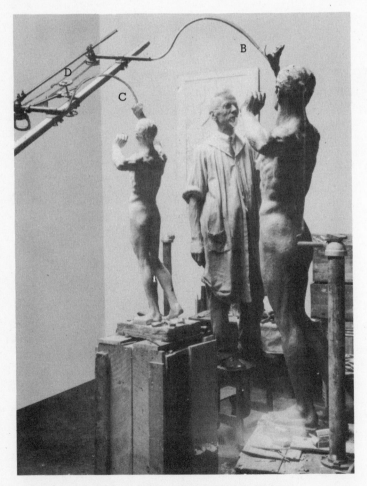

226. Enlarging Machine, Reul Type, Enlarging Small Model to Life-size Figure, "Nordic Type," by Malvina Hoffman, Hall of Man Collection, Field Museum, Chicago.

227. Scopas Student Enlarger Made by John Tiranti, London, 1938. On a Metal Tripod Stand the Complete Machine Is Attached Ready for Enlarging with Straight Pointers and Lead Counterweight. (BASIL)

XV. Photography and Lighting

ABOUT 1928 I made a most interesting experiment in photography. While studying the subjects who posed for their portraits, I had been frequently intrigued to discover the forms and lines that caused such a difference of expression on the two sides of a face. I was tempted to try out a sort of photographic analysis of the subject by taking a front view *exactly* in front of the model, so that the distance from a point in the center of the forehead to each ear would be exactly equal.

I made a print from this front-face negative. Then I made a print of the left side only. Reversing the negative and printing the same left side again gave me a face of two lefts. I then did the same with the right side of the face and got a print of two rights, making another face. If one sets these two composite faces beside the actual dissymmetrical front-view photograph, one is amazed by the revelation. If the character is made up of two very distinct or conflicting personalities, as is often the case, the surprising effects of the composite photographs will be more definite, while those who have grown up with strong will power controlling their emotional life, and great self-discipline, will show far less dissymmetrical formation.

I was fortunate in interesting a number of physicians and anthropologists in this experiment, and they were as astonished as I was to see themselves revealed so defenselessly by the simple trick of doubling each side of their face. Exact centering of the front view of the first photograph is absolutely necessary to obtain any sort of accurate registration. Otherwise the slightest deviation will result in distortion and false results. Some of those who posed for these experimental photographs advanced the theory that the left side of a face is what we are, and the right side is what we make of ourselves. It is an interesting subject for discussion.

There has been such remarkable progress of recent years in the field of photography that the results are frequently worthy of being called works of art. The student will do well to study the endless views of the human figure in athletics—diving, swimming, running, jumping, and the slow-motion films of all these actions and muscular effort of every kind. By closely studying photographs in the rotogravure newspaper supplements, the student can learn most valuable lessons about foreshortening perspective action poses, and appearance of the human figure and animals in every activity of life. It is often helpful to make sketches from such photographic records.

In the case of portrait photography the sculptor must learn just what tricks of distortion are played by the camera lens, and what retouching changes have been added to the original negative. For example, when studying a profile photograph from which one is asked to make a bas-relief, it is wise to have the unretouched negative whenever possible. Enlarge this to exactly life size; measuring from the chin tip to level of eyebrows is generally a safe area to take as a basis for proportions.

When this becomes life size it will be noted that the ear will be larger than life size, because it is the nearest part of the head to the camera and therefore not in the same plane as the profile outline, which is three or four inches further removed from the lens. Likewise, in the enlargement of a front-view photograph if the exact dimension is taken from chin to eyebrow, the nose will appear larger than life, because it is nearer the camera than the eyes.

To make the best use of photographs as guides to a portrait, it is well to place the sculpture in the same light as that in which the sitter was photographed. If the shadows on the sculpture appear too dark, it is generally because the lines or features are too deeply set. If the half tones in the modeling of the planes seem too pale, you must verify from front and side how to deepen the values by deepening the hollows. When working from two-dimensional pictures the sculptor must instinctively always consider the third dimension and imagine all the forms in section. Otherwise the result is often confused and the third-dimensional construction faulty.

Snapshots and even badly printed photographs can be of assistance if the sculptor has had enough experience to be forewarned of the dangers in relying upon two-dimensional guides. A good three-quarter view can often help to verify the line of a profile, by determining the projection of nose and lips from the facial plane as seen from that angle. Every minute detail in any view of a face can be of assistance in constructing a portrait either when the subject is unable to give the artist enough sittings or if the sculptor is making a portrait after death.

More Eggs. (L. MOHOLY-NAGY)

*228, 229. The Play of Light and Shade
on Flat and Rounded Surfaces:*

*Model Showing Crystal Formation Found
in Gems, Designed for Marcus & Co. by
W. B. Okie, Jr.*

230. *Interesting Patterns of Light and Shade on "The Column Without End,"
by Constantin Brancusi in the Public Garden in Targu Jiu, Rumania.*

(PHOTO BY BRANCUSI)

Photography has developed so many new and amazing possibilities that the sculptor naturally feels a great interest in how this new art may be used to interpret and reproduce sculpture. To give three-dimensioned quality to objects, a thorough knowledge of lighting and timing is essential.

To clarify this problem, an interesting experiment was made recently in the new Trocadéro Museum, Paris. There were some cases in which very fine old bas-reliefs were shown lighted from different angles, and figures in the round on slowly revolving pedestals revealed the astonishing effects of good and bad lighting. The correct placing of works of art is something that is very often treated with total indifference, although much more pleasure might be derived from marbles and bronzes if the owners would spend a little time and money on their suitable mounting, placing, and lighting.

It is a revelation to many what unthought-of qualities may be suddenly noticed when a well-installed, invisible beam of light is directed upon a marble or bronze or a terra cotta. The beam may be so controlled by a shutter of metal that only the actual object is illuminated and no surrounding circle of light or glare of any kind is visible.

To watch an artist of the caliber of Dr. Arnold Genthe or Mr. Moholy-Nagy taking photographs of sculpture is an education in itself: the patient experimenting with lights and shadows; the alertness with which they watch for sudden discoveries of hidden forms and silhouettes that spring to life under the sharp eye of a spotlight; what endless combinations of background, timing of exposures, and intensity of concentration needed to decide at just what split second the shutter must close and catch the image in the little magic box! These, and other artists of the camera, have helped to develop a new sense of light in the mind of man. They have captured and illuminated the fleeting phenomena of vision, and made the moment a permanent possession.

The success of the recent transformation of the badly lighted galleries of the Louvre, in Paris, into a new splendor of modern installation and indirect lighting has been proved by the vast crowds that instantly responded to this change. Masterpieces that were lost to view or crowded away into corners have come into a new era of their own. The marbles sparkle and turn on revolving pedestals; the bas-reliefs are sunk into the walls and lighted with soft, diffused reflectors which are hidden from sight. Even the little cards have been studied and remade. Transparent celluloid or synthetic glass cards, on which the legend is well printed, have taken the place of pasteboard or other material, with the result that the card itself is not noticeable, taking on by its transparency the color of the object behind it.

While visiting art galleries, it is interesting to note which ones have restful, yet adequate, lighting for the objects displayed. Light should be sensed but not seen. On account of the expense, naturally very few can afford lighting individual pieces by beam projectors hidden in the ceiling or woodwork; but more often than not, the long reflectors above our heads are so set that when looking at the pictures or sculpture near the walls the glare of the lights is also seen, and they are aimed so far downward that the baseboards of the side walls are brilliantly lighted. This is a serious error.

If we think of the complicated make-up on actors' and dancers' faces before they dare to step out on the stage in the glare of footlights, we may realize perhaps why so many portraits look so utterly strange and different when we see them in a house than when they were in our own studio. They are often placed on a high shelf, or over a bookcase, and the table lamp below is lighted. Suddenly the defenseless subject finds his marble countenance lit up from below, as in the case of the stage folk. His chin takes on a defiant, bright importance, also the underside of his nostrils and the projection under his eyebrows, leaving dark spots and caverns where in the studio top lighting he enjoyed the reverse of all these effects.

Have a heart, owners of art, and try to understand the problems of placing and lighting your treasures. The results will be rewarding and will double the interest on your investment.

XVI. *Plaster and Terra Cotta*

I T may be of interest to some of my readers, who have a certain curiosity about the hows, whys, and wherefores in the sculptor's profession to know how plaster is concocted, and how it is used in casting, and why it is well to understand its ingredients and limitations.

As usual when we dig down into the past, we find "the Greeks had a name for it." *Ge*, meaning the earth, *epsum*, meaning to concoct—hence "gypsum" (do not ask me why), which consists of a lime sulphate, and which is really the generic name for plaster.

I expect someone immediately to raise the question: "But why is it so often called plaster of Paris?" Because the earth under and around the city of Paris is exceptionally rich in this material, with an additional ten per cent of calcium. A great industry has been developed to manufacture and sell this product to the world.

Raw gypsum is calcium dihydrate ($CaSO_4.2H_2O$). This was originally used as a fertilizer, for sweetening the earth, and was known as land plaster.

The chalk cliffs of England, with which we are all so familiar, are a natural formation of calcium hemihydrate, or actual plaster. The ordinary chalk used for drawing on blackboards is made of this material, less dehydrated, however, and therefore softer than the ordinary hard plaster which results when it sets after being mixed with water.

Ordinary gypsum is found nearly everywhere in Europe and the Americas. The finest, most compact, and translucent quality is called alabaster. This is very soft stone, and is quite fragile.

The terra alba, or white earth, of France has been exported for centuries. It is dug out of the ground in great blocks; "boiled" or "baked" until all its moisture has evaporated; it is then ground up into fine powder in a mill. About twenty-five per cent of the original material is lost in its prepara-

255

231. Plaster-casting Tools. Left to Right, Standing: Pliers, Long Bristle Brush for Applying Plaster, Key Hole Chisel, Flat Chisel for Chipping, Plaster Knife for Cleaning Seams Etc., Steel Cutter, Two Clay Tools, Small Metal Tool (Round at One End, Pointed at the Other), Spatula with Rounded Ends, Spatula with Flat Ends (Both Used for Mixing and Working Plaster), Large Spatula with One End Saw-toothed, Bottle of Bluing, Bottle of Liquid Soap.

Foreground: Wooden Mallet, Tool for Bending Irons, Wooden Wedges and Wires, Mixing Bowls of Flexible Copper, Small Rubber Bowl (One-half of a Rubber Ball), Box of Paraffin Wax.

tion and evaporation. It should be kept always in a dry place, as dampness injures the plaster seriously. Plaster has served a useful purpose in reproducing numberless masterpieces of art, and in all manner of building construction—walls, ceilings, and decorative ornament. It is protection against fire hazards, and lends itself to a wide variety of treatment and surfacing.

It is generally conceded that "boiled" plaster is more reliable and less apt to warp than "baked" plaster. About three hours are needed to boil gypsum into the fine sandlike plaster, whereas sixteen hours are needed to dehydrate it by baking. If the oven is too hot, the plaster will lose its quality of absorption, which is of vital importance when it is used and mixed with water. If it is underbaked, it will set so quickly that it loses its value.

To test its consistency, squeeze a handful firmly. If it tends to keep its shape when the fingers release their pressure it is right; if it falls to pieces it has been exposed to dampness and is not reliable. It also feels like flour with soft, small lumps.

When mixed in water by sifting the powder evenly through the fingers, it should be carefully stirred from below, stirring in the same direction always, either by the hand or a large spoon. When the powder rises to the level of the water, let it stand a few moments, then stir slowly. Its consistency should be creamy and smooth. Avoid making air bubbles, and be sure not to leave any lumps. A good plaster mixture should set slowly and be very hard when dry. A quick-setting mixture (more powder and less water) is not so durable.

The chemical action, when plaster sets, is the change from the amorphous state of the sulphate of lime to crystallization. Adhesive strength of plaster is greatest when applied to its self; when applied to stone or iron its strength is slightly weakened. By mixing with lime water it becomes stronger and harder for building purposes.

Limestone is a rocky formation containing carbonate of lime as a base. In its purest and whitest form it is known as white marble. When iron or other colored minerals form its ingredients, the marble assumes other colors and veining. Lime water may be used to wash over plaster casts; it will harden the surface. It is also good to apply to cuts or bruises.

232. Group of Spatulas and Plaster-finishing Tools.

233. *Waste Mold of a Figure, Brass Shims Set Into the Clay Along the Line of the Seams.*

234. *Applying First Coat of Plaster to Back of Original Model, Using Long-haired Brush. Note Key Holes in Edge of Seam of Front Section Which Has Been Finished, and Also Note That the Hand Has Been Cut Off and Cast in a Separate Mold.*

235. *Part of Completed Mold Chipped Away, Showing the Finished Plaster Cast Inside, and Section of Mold with Dark Lines Showing Where Reinforcing Irons Were Set to Strengthen the Mold. These Are Removed Before the Rest of the Mold Is Chipped Off.*

Sometimes ox hair or goat hair is mixed with plaster or mortar to add strength and adhesion. Hemp and jute are also used for the same purpose with good results. Sand, which is formed of silica ground off quartz rocks, contains also a variety of metallic oxides. When it is mixed with lime and plaster, it serves to insure even mixtures and added resistance and reduces cost. When tremendous endurance is needed, however, pure cement is used, as the sand lessens the strength of cement. Portland cement is chiefly made up of carbonate of lime, alumina, and silica (from chalk, clay, or mud).

PLASTER WASTE MOLD
(Of a Bust, for Example)

1. Make a fence to divide the mold into front and back sections. Use either a clay strip or shims of brass firmly embedded in the clay and neatly overlapping each other to make an unbroken wall. Press about ½" into clay and leave a 2" projection outside. (If you have no brass use flat strip of clay ½" thick and 2" high.) Start at top of head center, and run down both sides back of ears. Do not put the fence too near the ears. If you use the clay strip, support it on the back by clay pieces as braces, 4 or 6 inches apart. Be sure front surface of fence is smooth and continuous.

2. Mix bowl of plaster sufficient for front section; color the water slightly with bluing before sifting in the plaster. Stir evenly and thoroughly to thick, creamy consistency.

3. Take a second small bowl, for easier handling, and scoop it full from the first supply of plaster. Hold this near the work to avoid spattering. Flick it with a backhanded motion against the face, beginning with eyes, nose, mouth, ears, and blow it into the deep undercuts before covering the rest of the face; work from top of head downward, leaving surface of this coating rough. Be sure all high points are well covered.

4. Clean off, while still soft, surplus plaster that has run down over wooden base. (Work neatly; it always saves time in the end.) Some casters wash over the first coating with clay water (but avoiding the parts near the fence and base) to facilitate chipping off the next coat. This is not necessary, however.

5. Prepare and bend your reinforcing irons while first coat is setting. Be sure to lay them around the seam area and from top to bottom in front of the face and laterally to save the mold from breaking (¼" square irons are convenient and adequate for a bust or small figure). A deep hole in a brick wall serves as a vise to bend irons (unless you have Herculean muscles).

236. *Reverse Negative of Plaster Mold Made on Quarter-size Model of International Dance Fountain. Note Effect of Top Lighting on Concave Forms, Giving Illusion of Positive Relief Lighted from Below. Vincent Russo, Plaster Caster.*

237. *Inside of Negative Plaster Mold Showing Irons Laid Against First Coat of the Positive Cast. These Will Be Covered by the Next Thick Coat of Plaster.*

238. *Iron Clamp for Holding Sections of Plaster Mold Together. This Does Away with the Necessity of Binding with Ropes, Wedges, Etc.*

6. The second coat is not colored but mixed thicker than the first. Flick on, as before, ½″ thickness. Set the irons in place. Tie them together with burlap dipped in plaster and pressed against second-coat surface. Press them just enough to hold up in the second coating.

7. When plaster is hard, remove clay fence. Drill key holes in surface of seam or put V-cuts at intervals along the outer edge of seam. This will assure perfect fit of back section, the plaster of which will run into the key holes or V-cuts and form the positive keys.

8. *Important:* Wash over this seam surface and key holes with clay water, so the fresh plaster will not stick.

9. Now mix a new bowl of plaster and repeat same operation for back section. When both coats are set, place flat chisel gently between the two sections at various points and wedge apart the molds. If it resists, drop a little water in the seam; this will facilitate removal of mold.

10. Take off back section first. Dig out clay *carefully.* (Do not scrape the inside of your mold!) To remove surplus clay that sticks in the under-cuts, take a lump of clay and press it against these pieces and pull out.

11. Wash molds and soap them until they will not absorb any more moisture (use green soap jelly, not hard soap). Apply with long, soft-haired brush and squeeze out brush to remove all surplus suds until surface is almost dry. Dip bristles of a dry brush in a little paraffin paste (diluted in turpentine) and cover molds lightly with this.

12. When this operation is completed, apply fresh plaster with soft brush over the entire surface of both sections, to avoid bubbles; be sure not to leave plaster on seams. Wait until plaster becomes thicker, not *hard,* and then assemble the two sections and bind them securely with strong cord and tighten with a stick. If you have ½″ iron clamps like that shown in figure 238, they replace the cord and save time.

13. Place mold upside down and pour in the remaining thick, creamy plaster. Mix fresh supply if necessary and continue until an even thickness of about ¾″ (for a bust) is assured over entire surface.

14. To reinforce neck, burlap strips or fiber dipped in plaster may be applied against inside surface as a lining.

15. When hard, begin to chip off the burlap ties and remove the irons. Continue to chip the outer mold with plaster chisel and wooden mallet until you see the *blue* coat appear; watch for this carefully! Proceed to chip more gently until you uncover the positive plaster model inside. Avoid letting the chisel edge cut or scratch the model, and if you do cut too deeply, mend these errors with very thin plaster while model is still wet. Smooth

off all trace of your mistakes without altering any of the original modeling.

When you make your first perfect cast you will have a feeling of joy and triumph.

METHOD OF CASTING A SIMPLE RELIEF

To cast a low relief where there are no undercuts, lay the relief flat on its back on the table and build a fence of clay strips all around it about one inch higher than the highest point of its relief. Into this pour smooth, creamy plaster until the entire relief is covered to about one-half-inch thickness. Over this lay strips of burlap and some strong galvanized wires, pressing them gently into the surface of the plaster. Reinforce the edges with stiffer plaster and let it set.

After removing the clay fences, the mold may be lifted off the relief.

The cast is made in the same manner as described for the other methods of plaster casting, by soaping, etc. If the relief is of large dimensions, it will be necessary to lay in strips of iron (one-quarter-inch iron, shellacked to avoid rust stains, is found useful for this purpose), following the shape of the outside edge of the frame, and one or two transverse pieces between these irons. They should be held together and reinforced by wads of fiber dipped in strong plaster and bound to the background of the cast. It is convenient to leave space between two of the irons and the background of the cast, so that wire loops may be attached by which to hang the finished relief.

METHOD OF MAKING A MOLD OF A HAND

1. Mix enough plaster for whole hand.
2. Put some of this in another bowl and stir slightly to speed up setting.
3. Dip hand in second mixture and take position desired.
4. Lay an oiled linen thread from side of wrist (after tying it there) along-side of hand and over the tops of all fingers and thumb at first joint from tips and along outside edge of thumb to other side of wrist.
5. When string is placed, use first bowl of plaster to cover and thicken mold.
6. Draw flat tool along surface over line where string is laid, to give clean, flat edges to seam when mold is separated.
7. When plaster is set (like *firm* but not *hard* butter) pull the string by the loose end along the same line that it was laid. Hold other end firmly.
8. When mold is ready to remove, shave outside surface of plaster, fol-

lowing line of seam only, with sharp knife, to give accurate line for the inside seam when the mold is put together.

9. When plaster is hard, separate the seams carefully with a wide plaster chisel. Lift off top and draw fingers carefully out of the mold.

METHOD OF MAKING A MOLD AND CASTING A COMPLETE HAND

1. The simplest method is to grease the hand inside and out, smoothing the hair flat.

2. Place in desired pose on a table. Block wrist with clay to prevent moving and keep plaster from running.

3. Build a clay fence three-quarters inch high, running around the hand. Make keyways (shallow dents) by pressing with tip of finger in this at intervals.

4. Mix plaster in warm water (tint with bluing). Be sure hand is not moved. Apply this as the first thin coat.

5. Add uncolored plaster, about one and one-half inches thick, quickly.

6. When set, turn hand and mold over carefully, without moving fingers in the mold.

7. Clean off clay fence, brush edges of plaster mold with clay water.

8. Mix fresh bowl of plaster with bluing. Cover inside of hand, thin coat, then quickly add one and one-half inch thick uncolored plaster and let it set.

9. Bend wrist slightly to open mold.

10. Fill in air bubbles if there are any.

11. Wires for fingers should be shellacked and dipped in plaster and left to dry, before inserting into the mold.

12. Mold should be thoroughly cleaned and soaped (use green soap, any drugstore can supply) with soft, long-haired brush; keep applying soap with continuous motion for about fifteen minutes. All bubbles and excess soap should be wiped off with dry brush, taking great care not to chip edges with wooden handle.

13. Oil surfaces of mold carefully and place wires in fingers before slowly pouring in fresh plaster (not tinted) to make the solid cast. Place wires in middle of each finger and set ends in palm with thick plaster, so they will not shift when plaster is poured in. No wires should come too near surface; always leave layer of plaster between surface and inside armatures. Use galvanized wire to avoid rust stains.

239. *Plaster Cast Showing How Leg Is Set in Place by a "Roman Joint." The Arm Is a Regular Keyed (Male and Female) Joint Used for Bronze Casting. The Female Section on the Upper Arm Holds the Key of Lower Arm, and a Metal Pin Transpierces Both and Holds Them Together. Monsieur Duhec at Rudier Foundry, Paris.*

240. *Group of Figures by Herbert Adams. Plaster Mold Being Chipped Off and Removed.* (DE WITT WARD)

241. *Running a Template. Preparation of Clay Core Covered with Wide-mesh Burlap Over Which Plaster Is Applied and to Which the Plaster Will Adhere When Finished. The Black Space Between the Zinc and the Burlap Indicates the Thickness of the Plaster, Which Will Be Applied as Shown in the Next Photograph.*

242. *Showing Method of Running Zinc Template to Make a Circular Bowl in Plaster. The Sheet of Zinc Is Attached to a Wooden Frame, the Top of Which Is Held on a Pivot Which Runs Down Through the Clay Core and Table Top Held in a Socket Below. By Pushing the Wooden Frame Around the Model on a Flat Table, the Surface of the Soft Plaster Is Shaved Off, Leaving a Silhouette Exactly Like the Edge Cut in the Zinc Template. If Any Holes or Rough Spots Are Left After the First Turning, These Must Be Filled and the Template Turned Until the Surface Is Perfect. When the Plaster Has Set It Is Lifted Off and the Clay Core Removed, Leaving a Hollow Cast Reinforced by the Burlap Lining.*

ANOTHER METHOD OF MAKING A MOLD

Grease the skin thoroughly, smoothing down the hairs in the direction that they grow. Dip the hand in a bowl of creamy plaster, lift out, and take desired pose of fingers, etc., bracing wrist to prevent any movement. As the plaster sets, lay a strong thread greased with oil lightly on this first layer (do not press it onto skin) from wrist over tip of third finger, along center of palm to the wrist; leave long ends. Do not move the fingers after this. Lay another thread from wrist along outside of thumb over the tip and back to the inside wrist; leave end free. Cover with plaster, thickness about three-quarters of an inch. When plaster sets, but not too firmly, pull steadily on two ends of threads. This will cut the seams of the piece molds. Wait for setting hard before taking the pieces off.

If only the top of a hand is molded, it may be laid on a board and padded with clay below to prevent the plaster from running under the edges. Lay a fence of clay around the hand one inch away from the edges, to prevent plaster from running over the board. When the plaster covering is set, the fingers may be moved ever so gently and slowly to release them from the casing, while the mold is steadily pulled off the hand.

The cast is made as described in the other methods.

MASKS FROM LIFE

Dr. Flinders Petrie has found evidence to prove that molds were made from living subjects even as far back as 1300 B.C.

Various methods have been used, but a simple one is as follows. Let the model sit up in a comfortable armchair. Tie a cloth over his hair to edge of brow; tie it tightly at back of head. Cover his shoulders and arms well with towels, and roll one closely around the neck to prevent the plaster from running down; cover this with oiled paper securely to form a sort of gully, not rising too high to interfere with casting chin and ears.

If the subject has a beard or mustache, cover these with a coating of clay paste. Rub the eyebrows and eyelashes with vaseline, or cover with boiled starch paste if you have no vaseline. Plug the ears carefully with cotton wool. Set two strong quills on the nostrils, holding them firmly in place with cotton wool; do not use straw tubes, as they often bend under the weight of plaster and thus automatically cut off the air. In such a case the model signals violently that he cannot breathe, and the plaster must immediately be removed from the nose area and the nostrils cleared. New tubes must then be inserted as before. All this frightens the subject unnecessarily and causes delay and probably injury to the mold.

The face should be greased evenly all over before applying the first thin layer of plaster. This should be mixed with warm water and applied quickly. Lay oiled linen thread on this thin coat, dividing the face into two halves. Another bowl of plaster should be in readiness, mixed with water and alum (or salt) to set more quickly. Apply this thicker over the thread. When this outer layer is as hard as butter, pull end of thread, holding the other end firmly. When hard, wedge the seam apart gently with a wide chisel. Take off one section at a time. The first layer, next to the skin, will not have set so fast; therefore it will not pull out the hair of the eyelashes and brows—at least we hope it won't!

If the hair has attached itself to the plaster, the victim must practice mind control and cheerfully submit to being "plucked," realizing that he is making his offering to the cause of art, science, or experience, whichever it may be. He must not move his muscles or even laugh at the idea, as the mold will be damaged. The fact that it grows hot as it hardens should not alarm him, if he is told of it in advance.

It is seldom that one finds a subject willing to have both the front and back of his head cast, but if this rara avis does wish it done, he can patiently allow the molder to proceed. His neck will be tired, so he can remove the front mold. The edges must be cleaned and keyways cut in them and washed with clay water. This mold can be braced in a wooden frame on a table, and the subject can lean over and fit his face into the mold, the quills having been removed and holes cleared for his breathing. For strangely enough, the encased living model must be allowed to continue breathing.

The caster then applies the plaster to the back of the head and neck, having greased the hair and mixed the first-layer plaster with warm water and the second with alum and salt water. If cold water is used the skin automatically gets chilled and the surface is goose flesh; the hairs stand up, and all this injures the surface of the plaster mold. When plaster has set, the back section is lifted off and the victim liberated.

After the two sections are cleaned, soaped, and oiled, a cast can be made of the complete head. This often bears little real resemblance to the model except for the bony construction. So let's call the whole thing off, it's such a disagreeable experience!

Of course all masks are not made in exactly the same manner. They can be done in one mixing of plaster. It is more likely, however, to pull out the hairs. The subject may also lie down, his head on a board to support the plaster, which is heavier than most people realize and may cause the subject great fatigue. This is perhaps the best way to avoid discomfort.

It is at best a very unpleasant ordeal but sometimes necessary, and if done by experts it is not dangerous. Every beginner should practice on hands or feet and grow familiar with all the problems before attempting a head of his best friend. There have been unfortunate incidents when the subject, not realizing that the plaster would get hot and heavy, has become frightened or faint. This occurred with certain athletes and polo players. On the other hand, a Hawaiian man I met in Honolulu submitted his entire body to be molded as well as his head; but this was a real endurance test, for the sake of science, which he would never be willing to repeat. If serious mistakes are made by inexperienced molders, the results may prove fatal to the subject.

SIMPLEST WAY TO MAKE A COMPLETE HEAD AND DEATH MASK IN TWO PIECES, USING THREAD

1. Be sure everything is well supported and steady before starting to work.
2. Brace back of head on a block of wood.
3. Cover neck and shoulders with cloths, so that no trace of plaster will be left when the work is finished.
4. Grease the face, eyelashes, eyebrows (mustache and beard, if any) carefully with vaseline. Smooth down the hair and grease this thoroughly, otherwise it will stick to the plaster. Plug the nostrils and ears with cotton wool. Do not force it in, and be sure not to change the shape of the nostrils when doing this.
5. Mix plaster enough for covering whole head.
6. Put part of the plaster in a separate bowl, and use this for first coat. Place greased thread beginning at neck front following profile and over center of head down to back of neck. Leave long ends out.
7. Add remaining layer of plaster from original bowl (about one and one-half inches, and slightly thicker over thread for strengthening seam area). When set to the consistency of firm butter, pull one end of thread, holding the other so it will not slide through.
8. Let plaster set. Scratch surface to be sure it is hard. Insert flat chisel between edges of the seam, and gently wedge it open. Set two pieces of

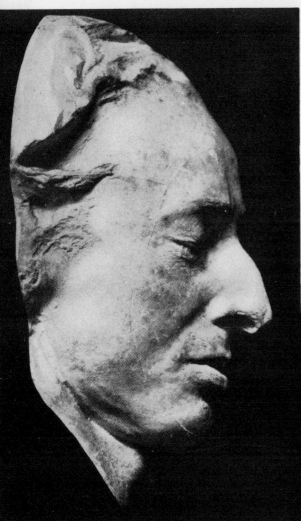

243. Death Mask of Frédéric Chopin.
(FROM "DAS LETZTE GESICHT," ED. DR. EMIL SCHAEFFER)

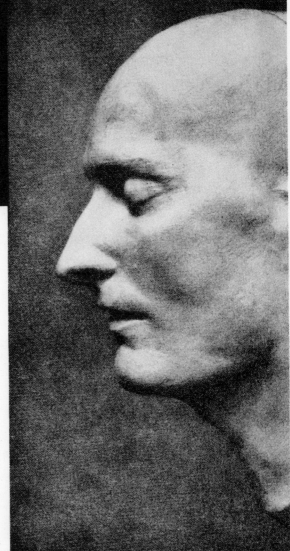

244. Death Mask of Napoleon.
(FROM "UNDYING FACES," BY ERNST BENKARD)

245. *Drawing of John Keats Made by M. H., 1910, in the Room Where Keats Died, Piazza di Spagna, Rome.*

mold carefully together; avoid chipping seam edges. Lock the two molds together with burlap or jute dipped in plaster.

9. Be careful to remove all traces of your plaster work. When finished take the cotton from nostrils and ears; wipe the grease off and arrange the subject exactly as you found him. A wad of cotton dipped in natural-color powder sometimes takes away any shine of the grease.

DEATH MASKS INCLUDING EARS
(*Method Using Clay Fence*)

The ears should be plugged with cotton wool and supported from underneath with cotton or clay. Plug the nostrils carefully. A clay fence can be set down the center of the face from top of brow to the neck. The hair, eyebrows, and eyelashes must be thoroughly greased and smoothed as flat as possible, likewise the edges of the hair which may not be covered by the cloth bound around the head and tied firmly behind the ears at the back. In the case of a mustache, clay paste can be applied so that the natural form is retained in the mold.

Mix plaster in cold water. When one side of the face has been covered, let it set (make it slightly thicker along the seam and smooth this surface). Remove the clay fence, cut some keyways in the upper edge of the seam, wash the seam with clay water, and apply the plaster for the other half of face. Open carefully and draw gently to release the ears. Dry off all traces of grease from the hair and eyebrows, etc.; be careful never to leave any trace of plaster or any mark whatever on the subject. Sometimes a little talcum powder on a wad of cotton removes all the shine of the oil.

POST-MORTEM PORTRAITS

Here there are many difficulties for the sculptor to overcome. When the family have had the foresight to have a plaster mask taken immediately after death, they often feel that from this reproduction of the facial forms and features the sculptor should be able to produce a living likeness with little effort.

In the first place, there are comparatively few good masks made. The forms have generally been flattened and deformed by the weight of the plaster, or because of nervousness on the part of the person taking the mask. If, however, the mask is good, there is the possibility of verifying all the proportions and bony structure of the head.

The artist must have studied the inevitable changes that take place immediately after death, and be familiar with just what parts of the face are most likely to have been distorted either by the pressure of plaster, or by the embalming processes.

When all the measurements are verified it is well to put away the mask and work entirely from photographs, or from memory if the subject was known to the sculptor. This will avoid the great danger of having any suggestion of the death mask in the portrait, which would be fatal. I am afraid it is only by repeating the experience very often that one can successfully evoke a living and convincing portrait either from photographs or from death masks.

After studying hundreds of photographs one gradually learns how to read them in terms of three dimensions, and the mind instantaneously considers what happens around the corner from the view which is actually presented in the picture; in this way the dynamic living quality of the artist is infused into the work, and the result is a sort of evocation of a personality rather than an exact likeness. The family is often led astray by too many photographs when criticizing the sculptor's interpretation. They are tempted to judge each view of the head from the various views of the pictures, not realizing that the sculptor's task is to absorb all these views and synthesize them in a whole that will be convincing, and not to reproduce exactly any one photographic impression, which would only be possible in two dimensions, and would be of very transitory interest.

It is, after all, the spirit and character of a personality that should be felt in a good portrait, and above all these demands, the responsibility of the sculptor is to make of this portrait a work of art.

MAKING A PIECE MOLD

First Method

Plaster must be mixed thin to prevent expansion. A pinch of salt will make it set faster.

When a complicated piece mold is needed, each piece should be numbered or marked so that it will fit into its correct place. All joints should be brushed with soap solution before the next section is made. All edges are made at an angle which will permit the piece to be drawn away without damaging the edges.

Roll out strips of firm clay and cut them about one-half inch thick and wide to make the fences for the pieces; be sure they are clean and smooth. Begin to set them on the model from the bottom upward. After setting the fence, brush on sweet oil or suet solution over the section of model to be cast.

Apply the plaster and let it set. Take off the fence, take off the plaster piece, clean the edges, and refit it into place to be sure it is perfect. Tap lightly if necessary. Set a new fence for the next piece. Repeat the oiling for each section, and soap the edge of the finished piece. When the pieces are set, shellac and grease entire outer surface of these. Make an outside case of plaster over them to hold all in place. If the model is round, make two half sections with keyways in outer case seam. On pieces of the back section, insert wire loops, and cut holes through the casing at these points. A string is now tied to each wire loop and passed through a hole cut through the outer casing. This string is tied to a little stick which may be turned until the piece is firmly held. This is done so the inside pieces will not fall out when the back of the mold is turned over the front section. Set the two sections of casing together and tie them up tightly with strong rope.

1. To clean and soap the negative molds: boil a pint of water and add two tablespoonfuls of green soap (unadulterated); boil until well dissolved; keep in a corked bottle.

2. Do not use hard soap; the cast will never be as sharp or crisp as when boiled soap is used. It may be hot or cold, but not too thick.

3. Be sure the brush has soft, long bristles. Do not chip the edge of the molds with the handle of brush. Soap them for fifteen minutes, or more if they are wet molds.

4. Pour off liquid, and after a few minutes brush off surplus soap carefully by squeezing the same brush to absorb all superfluous liquid.

5. Take a dry brush and rub its ends in olive oil, in the palm of your hand. Do not leave bubbles or drops of oil on brush.

6. Go over entire surface of molds, giving them a smooth, shiny surface.

7. Dip molds in water or play a syringe over them until they are thoroughly wet throughout. This will prevent air holes in the cast, which can cause great inconvenience.

8. Leave molds to dry and tie them together again with tight cords. Set them upside down on the floor to be filled.

9. Mix plaster to creamy consistency and pour in a bowlful. Rotate, and turn the complete mold in every direction. When inner layer is all covered, pour in a second and third bowl of plaster until an even thickness of ½″ or so is on all the surfaces.

10. Jute fiber or burlap may be pressed in wads against the inside of neck if strengthening there is needed.

11. Leave all to set firmly.

12. Take off outer shell carefully; watch it. Replace each piece in its place in the shell.

Second Method (*Without Clay Fences*)

Start making pieces below, working upward as each piece is made. Take off, shave off smooth seam surface with a knife, replace on the plaster model and grease the surface before making the next piece, and soap the seam or wash with clay water, always selecting the largest possible section that will surely "draw" without damaging the model's surface. It is convenient to make a small key piece with a wire loop which is lifted out first and facilitates removing the adjacent pieces. When all pieces are made, the outside surface should be smoothed and greased, and an outer two-piece shell (front and back) made over all. Each piece on the back should be tied through the shell so that it will not fall out when turned over the front section for casting.

GELATINE MOLD

If more than one plaster cast is needed of the same subject, the usual process is to make a jelly mold. It is pliable, strong, and easily drawn off the plaster model even when there are undercuts.

1. The best rubber jelly is recommended, or Japanese gelatine.

2. After soaking in cold water until soft, put it in a gluepot (first oiling this).

3. Immerse pot in water the level of which must be higher than the jelly in the pot, to prevent top jelly from burning.

4. Place stirring stick in jelly through a hole in the pot cover. Jelly pot should not touch bottom of water pot. Let water circulate under it; put three or four bricks, or perforated dish pan, to support its weight.

5. Heat slowly over gas ring until liquid.

6. Prepare plaster cast with coating of white shellac. When dry, oil this to avoid sticking; attach it to the stand so it will not move; mark outline in pencil on stand to be perfectly sure.

7. Roll out well-kneaded clay about ¾" thick, cover model with this all over, pressing it firmly to avoid bulging; leave it thicker where the seam is to be located.

8. Put extra cone-shaped knobs of clay at intervals on the surface about 2" high. Be sure these are over the high points of the model, for they serve as air vents later on when jelly is poured in.

9. Place clay fence about 2" high up the sides and over the top. In the

top center of the fence leave a separate clay plug, 1½" in diameter, which will be your funnel opening for pouring jelly into the plaster casing. Brace the fence on front surface with triangular pieces of clay.

10. Apply plaster to back section, covering smooth clay surface evenly to about 1" in thickness, or more if needed. Let it set.

11. Remove clay fence, and cut keyways in plaster edge of casing. Clean and soap these, or oil them.

12. Apply front section of plaster, same thickness. Clean off neat seams and general surface. Screw strips of wood around casing on the stand. (This will insure exact replacing of mold when clay lining has been removed.)

13. Mark F on front and B on back half. Unscrew the wood strips on the stand. Wedge open the casing, clear out the clay, clean the mold, and see that the cone key holes go through the casing, for these act as air vents when jelly is poured in.

14. After cleaning, shellac the inside of the casing and rub over with paraffin on rag or soft brush.

15. Brush over the plaster model with paraffin. See that its position has not shifted on your penciled outline. Screw the wood strips for the section exactly in original position.

16. Set back of plaster casing into position.

17. Fit the front section carefully into the keyways of the back, and screw down the wood strips.

18. Bind the two sections tightly with rope and wedge, and nail rope ends down to wooden base; otherwise the mold will rise up when jelly is poured in.

19. All this time the gelatine has been heating. Now you turn off the gas, and let the gelatine cool off until you can hold your finger in it. A skin forms on top.

20. Be sure not to pour it into the mold when too hot. It will melt the shellac covering on the plaster cast and stick to the model.

21. Instead of water, vinegar can be used to dissolve the jelly, and it will be more elastic and durable.

22. If new gelatine is used, skim off the top before pouring, as pieces may break off and fall into mold. If gelatine is old put a funnel in hole at top left by clay plug, and pour slowly, leaving skin over top of jelly. This skin keeps the jelly hot and fluid for a longer time. Make two holes in it, one on top and one nearer the lower rim. As you turn the pot over, do not tip too quickly.

23. An assistant should help now, and have a few lumps of clay handy and watch the air holes carefully. When the jelly runs out of the hole freely, he should plug it up with clay. As the jelly rises inside, each hole must be plugged firmly after jelly runs out. Fill the mold until the jelly rises to the top of the funnel. Watch it! If an air hole plug comes out, plug it again, and see that the level of the jelly has not lowered. Refill if necessary.

24. When jelly has begun to set well, take off funnel and cut off the jelly to level of the plaster casing. Leave it all night to set before opening.

25. Remove the front section of casing, and divide the jelly mold with a jelly knife which makes a grooved joint seam, drawing it down along the edge of the back section seam. Then remove back casing. Pull the jelly molds carefully away from the plaster model inside.

26. Dust the outside of the jelly molds and the lining of the plaster casing with French chalk. Keep the jelly always in its case.

27. Wash out inside of jelly molds with a solution of alum and water, edges also. Brush over with paraffin; a few drops only are needed to dampen the brush.

28. Fit the keyways together and bind up the two sections firmly, with jelly lining inside.

29. Pour in plaster of thick creamy consistency; it is absolutely necessary to mix it with cold water.

30. Turn the mold in all directions so that the plaster will be sure to flow into all the corners and undercuts. Keep on adding plaster until desired thickness of cast is obtained.

31. Let it set. Then lay the mold flat and take off front section first, lifting jelly by lower edge of base. Dust this on outside with French chalk again and reset it in its casing. See that all the air vent cone points are in good shape. Do the same with back section.

PIECE MOLDS IN WAX

The surface of the model, either plaster, terra cotta, or marble, should be dusted with French chalk to prevent adhesion and possible discoloring. Each wax piece must be dusted on its joints and the whole held in place by an exterior shell of plaster, following the same method as described for plaster piece molds. The reason for using wax on a valuable or unique original model is to obviate any possible damage to the details on the fragile original.

1. ½ lb. of pure beeswax ⎫ Melt over slow heat; add about one pound
  ½ lb. of lard   ⎬ of flour, slowly mixing it in and stirring thor-
  1 gill linseed oil   ⎭ oughly.
2. Paraffin wax, olive oil, whiting. Same proportion as above. Pour out
on flat table and work it all together like dough until the consistency
is even and pliable.

TO HARDEN THE SURFACE AND WEATHERPROOF PLASTER CASTS

To harden the surface of plaster casts, they may be soaked in hot paraffin
or thoroughly brushed over with a melted solution of stearine. When dry,
the surface may be rubbed to a high polish. For large figures or reliefs in
plaster to be set out of doors, after the plaster has been thoroughly dried it
is brushed over inside and out with linseed oil, two or three coats. When
this has penetrated all the pores and hardened the surface, the plaster may
be painted with waterproof paint, and it may finally be colored to imitate
stone or bronze; it should be able to withstand exposure out of doors for
two years.

If you mix carefully skimmed milk with the water, before sifting in the
plaster, your cast will have a surface which, after thorough drying, may
be rubbed to a polish.

When the plaster is clean and dry, it can be coated with hot, white wax,
left to absorb, and rubbed with a clean woolen cloth.

CARE OF PLASTER

If you happen to be a traveling sculptor in the tropics and need to cast
your own work, you may find out that where plaster is exposed to moisture
or damp climate, it becomes quite useless. When I was in Bali and the
Malay jungles, the rainy season added a few problems to the preservation
of plaster. It had to be sealed in hermetically divided metal containers. Each
section had a sheet of tin soldered around the inside of the can, so that I
could use the necessary amount for casting a head without exposing the
rest of my supply. If, however, you do not happen to have thought this out
beforehand, and all you can find is dead, evaporated plaster, you *may* be
able to use it if you put it in a big pot over a fire and keep stirring constantly. It must not burn, but merely evaporate its moisture.

MENDING BROKEN PLASTER CASTS

Mix plaster very weak (less plaster, more water). Let it stand a few minutes without stirring. Use directly on water-soaked surfaces of the broken plaster model, and brace these so no movement whatever takes place while setting.

To avoid the slight difference in color, when retouching is necessary, mix equal parts of plaster and water, and stir thoroughly. Leave it a few minutes, pour off surplus water, and use this directly without mixing further. Keep a bowl of water handy and a soft brush for smoothing the final surface.

CASTING IN NEGOCOLL

Inaugurated by Dr. Poller in Vienna

The elastic plastic quality of this material makes it a valuable substitute for plaster. When heated in a double boiler, it melts, and when applied very warm to the skin (no greasing is necessary), it gradually cools and hardens into a strong yet slightly pliable mold. This can be removed from a hand, for instance, in one piece avoiding any seams or joints and needing no retouching whatever. Either plaster or "hominit" may be used for the positive cast. All information and the materials for this process may be obtained from Kern & Co., 136 Liberty Street, New York City.

VARIOUS METHODS OF COLORING PLASTER CASTS

To Imitate Bronze

1. Always be sure that the cast is perfectly dry.

Paint it over with thin, even coat of shellac. If this is too thick, use wood alcohol to dilute it.

Let this dry.

Mix dry color of general tone desired in shellac. Paint this with soft brush over entire surface, quickly.

When dry, mix bronze powder in a little floor wax paste. Dab this lightly over the model with cloth pad and brush, touching all the parts you wish to accent and stippling the surface, so the bronze does not stay in spots.

Let this set for the night, or until the surface is dry, and then polish with flannel cloth. If extra high lights are needed, retouch with the wax mixed with golden bronze.

Any number of good results may be obtained in this manner.

2. *Another way is:*

After the first coat of shellac is dry, mix dry or oil color with turpentine, so that it will give a good, even covering of foundation tone—light green, for example. Leave it until the surface is just a little "tacky."

In a bowl, stir talcum powder and dry colors of gray and green until thoroughly mixed. Dust this lightly onto the model, with very soft camel's-hair brush, watching to make sure it is sticking to the tacky surface.

For effects of varied metallic patine, when the colored surface is dry mix bronze powder with soft wax paste, and touch up high spots with this. Then add a little real dust and talcum for grayish accents, and rub, when entirely dry, with a soft cloth.

Any color of bronze may be imitated in this coloring process, but experience and practice are needed to know when to start and stop each stage of the work, and how much accenting of the high lights is necessary.

3. *Another method:* After plaster is absolutely dry, dilute glue in water, very thin mixture; add a little Prussian blue powder, black, and yellow ocher. Cover surface thoroughly, but not too thick, with soft brushing in several coats. If too dark or too even, add color, always thin. When last one is still tacky, dip ends of soft, dry brush in dark gold powder; dab this lightly on all high spots, drapery, etc., according to taste. When thoroughly dry, rub gently with flannel.

4. *Fourth method:* Brush over a coat of bronze varnish. Let dry. In second coat mix raw umber and burnt sienna and a little white (dry color powders). Let this dry.

An oil varnish may be applied after this, and when almost dry, dust on, with soft brush, golden bronze finely powdered.

Paper or cardboard may be coated with white of egg or varnish mixed with alcohol. When tacky, dust on desired tones of bronze or gold powder on a tampon of cotton wool, and stipple over with soft brush. When dry, polish lightly.

To Imitate Silver

Paint on, when plaster is thoroughly dry, equal parts mercury and bismuth of zinc, and cover with varnish.

To Imitate Porphyry, Granite, Etc.

The plaster surface may be worked over with stone-carving tools before applying the first coat of shellac to give even a more convincing effect of stone or granite.

Mix desired oil color rather thin, cover surface, and let dry. Imitate veins or lines with fine brush. (Copy a small sample, for practice.) When almost dry, dip a stippling brush (bushy, round brush, ends cut off) in a tone of dark reddish color to dapple an all-over pink ground, or bluish for dappling over gray underpainting, depending on the sample you wish to imitate. Let this dry thoroughly. Spray entire surface with siccative varnish or thinned shellac. If you wish to add a little sparkle to imitate granite, pulverize mica and stipple this on lightly, mixed with shellac, or dip a whisk broom in it and draw a stick over bristles. This will serve as a spray. If you mix pulverized plate glass with superfine plaster, the effect of white marble is obtained.

By using a spray instead of a brush, very fine variations of shading may be obtained and all traces of brush marks are avoided. Be sure to clean the spray with alcohol if shellac has been blown through it, or with turpentine if oil color has been used. If oil or shellac is left to dry in it, the spray will become clogged and be useless. For large work a compressed-airbrush spray is a great timesaver.

BRETHAUER METHOD OF MAKING WEATHERPROOF PLASTER CASTS

Mix pulverized lime in water to the consistency of a paste. Add plaster and mix thoroughly. Cast the figure. When dry, paint with hot linseed oil, several coats. Varnish this thoroughly with linseed oil varnish. Paint the entire surface with good oil paint. This should withstand weather three or four years.

If you mix powdered pumice stone and plaster, equal amounts of each, you can cast a mold strong enough to resist the heat of molten metal.

CLEANING PLASTER

Dirty old casts may be cleaned by covering them with a layer of starch paste. When almost dry, peel off carefully. Dirty plaster may also be washed, but *not* in the ordinary manner. The cast must be submerged entirely under water and left to soak. While still submerged, a sponge may be rubbed over the surface lightly. The dust will loosen and float on top of the water. Every particle of this must be lifted off on a blotter, and when no sign of dust is seen, the cast may be removed and left to dry in a dustproof place. A thin coat of white shellac may be applied later, which makes a stronger and easier surface to keep clean.

246. *Exterior View of Terra Cotta Kilns, Atlantic Terra Cotta Co., Perth Amboy, N. J.* (F. S. LINCOLN)

247. *Interior of Terra Cotta Kiln, Showing How the Terra Cotta Models Are Loaded Into the Oven to Be Baked.* (F. S. LINCOLN)

TERRA COTTA

Terra cotta is clay baked in a kiln or oven. This treatment of clay dates back to antiquity and seems to give it an almost everlasting endurance. Mineral colors are sometimes applied to the surface when the clay is dry and hard, before baking, and these pigments are permanent.

Rare old examples of terra cotta vases and ornament have been found in Babylon, Persia, and China. When traveling northwest of Hong Kong, recently, I visited some excavations and enjoyed digging among the rocks and finding fragments of terra cotta bowls of a remote period. One piece had a raised design of a swastika clearly modeled on its outer surface.

Egypt, Greece, and Etruria also excelled in this art. The British Museum exhibits Etruscan terra cotta sarcophagi on which are modeled recumbent figures of exceptional beauty.

It is well for the sculptor who plans to work in this medium to know that the clay must be of a smooth and even texture, so that the firing will result in equal hardness and uniformity; otherwise the forms twist in the baking or, by warping, lose their original shape. The ideal mixture of clay for larger models must include one-third previously burnt clay or grit; this is known as grog. The sculptor may, by modeling his idea directly in potter's clay, dispense with plaster casting and bake his original model. He must build it solid, without any armatures, and hollow it out evenly from within when completed.

Sometimes it is advisable, when building up a figure, to cut a section out of the back all the way down to the base, with a wire tool, keeping the edges very sharp and clean. At this opening it is possible to hollow out the figure to an even thickness of about one inch, or more if the figure is large. The edges of the opening must be washed over with fine clay paste and the back piece reset in position. It is readily understood that if the thickness of the cast is very uneven, the shrinkage of the clay will also be uneven and may cause cracking during the firing. Likewise, if any piece of metal is used as an inside support, firing will expand it and crack the mold; and if wood is used, the heat will completely destroy it and result in damaging the figure.

When many replicas of a terra cotta are needed, the original clay must be cast in a plaster piece mold; the potter's clay is then pressed or squeezed into this negative mold. Great care must be taken that the clay be compact and not too wet. The fingers must press evenly and in a continuous sequence

248. Terra Cotta Warrior, 6th century Etruscan, Metropolitan Museum.

of motion, so that each piece when applied becomes an integral part of the previous one. No air spaces must be permitted in any part of the squeeze of clay. This sounds like a very simple operation, but in actual fact it takes a great deal of practice for perfect results to be obtained.

To facilitate removing the piece mold from the outer surface of the pressed clay, it is advisable to dust over the dry negative mold with talcum powder, blowing out any residuary particles before putting in the clay. This is, however, not a necessary procedure.

After a number of replicas have been pressed into the mold, this should again be dried thoroughly, as the plaster naturally absorbs some of the water from the clay at each pressing. After the pieces have been removed, the surface seam marks on the clay should be retouched, and the sculptor may at this time add any additional crispness to the detail before it is actually baked in the oven.

A wet clay solution (like heavy cream) may be *poured* into plaster instead of being pressed in. The water in the clay is absorbed by the plaster mold, but the inside clay stays wet and allows the next layer to adhere and become a part of it, until the needed thickness is obtained. Terra cotta casts must be thoroughly dried in an even temperature before baking. If left outdoors in the hot sun they are liable to crack. When the casts are large, supporting clay buttresses may be placed against them for safety, while drying.

Kilns, or furnaces, are built of fire bricks bound securely with iron bands bolted together. Each cast must be separated from the others when loaded into the oven. Small objects can be placed on fire bricks allowing the hot air to circulate freely. A few flat wads of clay may be set in the oven on fire bricks to test the heat. Take these out at intervals to insure the correct time to bake the original models.

When the kiln is filled, the opening is bricked up with fire bricks and iron bands bolted over it. No flames should ever touch the models. Fires must be watched and kept at a steady heat, sometimes for three or four days. Avoid excessive heat, which will burn the clay. The cooling off takes longer and must be done very slowly; the kiln is kept closed, for a sudden chill would crack the terra cotta. The clay, after baking, should have shrunk quite uniformly about one-twelfth of its original size.

The different clays used determine the color of the terra cottas. The uniform buff color needs a long baking and expert firing.

No one should attempt this work without having a thorough training or doing it under the direction of an experienced terra cotta molder.

Ordinary building bricks are of course made of baked clay or terra cotta and may be ground up, mixed with a little binder or cement, and cast into molds of heads or other subjects. The result is often very interesting and pleasing in color and texture. The surfaces of brick walls may also be carved and decorated after the walls are dry and the bricks well set. The courses of brick will naturally be evident, but if the design is simple and rugged enough, this will not detract from the final effect. A good recent example of this method is the relief by Katharine Lane on the Harvard Biological Building.

METHOD OF COLORING TERRA COTTA

A simple way is to mix the desired tone (in dry color powder) with raw milk and then paint this evenly over the surface. When thoroughly dry, it can be rubbed gently to give the effect desired.

Another way of coloring terra cotta: Fill an earthenware flower pot with sand. Put small terra cotta inside this, entirely covering it. Every other day soak the sand with one-half milk, one-half water mixture for about two weeks.

Feldspar or ground-up rock, mixed with certain clays, forms the base for high-fire glazes (2300°).

Real gold powder mixed with varnish may be sprayed on clay baked once. Then the second firing of 1200° burns away the varnish and fuses the gold into the surface of the terra cotta, producing "fire gilding."

Oxide of lead and tin, called opacifile, has been used since ancient times for opaque coloring of terra cottas, with fine effect.

TERRA COTTA WALLS

If the interior surface of brick walls has been discolored by dampness, this area may be cleaned off with a wire brush and painted with coal tar mixed with a solution of paraffin: one part paraffin to three parts coal tar oil, mixed *warm* and kept warm by sinking the pot in a hot-water container. Be sure the bricks are dry before applying this. Two coats may be put on if the place is exposed to weather on the outside wall. This may then be painted with oil colors or cement paint.

249. *Polychrome Terra Cotta Figures by Paul Jennewein, Philadelphia Art Museum.* (NEWELL)

250. *Frieze by Katharine Lane, Carved Directly on the Brick Wall of the Biological Laboratory, Harvard University.* (PAUL WEBER)

SUGGESTED FORMULA FOR CASTING CEMENT

Usual proportions: 3 parts sand, 1 part cement, mixed with marble dust according to brilliance required.

If colored effects are desired mix sand, marble dust, cement, and mineral color thoroughly. The sand must be absolutely dry. When all has been thoroughly mixed, sift it through a fine wire screen, so the material is very fine. The quantity for the entire job should be prepared at one time so the color will be uniform. A mask should be worn while mixing and sifting as the dust is suffocating.

Add the water as required, only enough for each day's work, as any excess mixture will set during the night and be useless for further work.

Coloring cement for out of doors: When the cement cast is about three weeks old, wash over the surface with sulphuric acid and water, or one-quarter pound of ammonia salt in nine quarts of water. It is best to use casein paint: 3 parts cheese, 1 part slaked lime, mixed thoroughly with whatever dry color powder is desired. Use only earth colors or oxides of iron. Never use inorganic colors or aniline dyes, white leads or Prussian blue. Oil paint will crackle off cement or lose its even tone of color.

251. "The Slipper," Majolica or Glazed Terra Cotta Figure by E. O. de Rosales.

252. *Statuette in Polychrome Terra Cotta by Alexandre Archipenko.*

253. *"Caryatid," by Rodin, Terra Cotta, Metropolitan Museum.*

XVII. Bronze

IT may be a surprise to many of my readers to learn that the art of casting bronzes in the cire-perdue—lost-wax—method was only developed seriously as an industry in America as recently as 1900.

About that time there was a foundry on West 25th Street in New York where men were experimenting with the lost-wax process. But the sculptors of that day did not evince any interest in the project, and the results were not very satisfactory.

It generally takes the enthusiasm of some one person to push over any pioneering work of this kind. In this case, great credit is due to the efforts and tenacity of Riccardo Bertelli, who came to America from Italy with the great dream of introducing and developing the art of cire-perdue casting; here, he thought, it might be advanced to a high standard because of the scientific progress in metallurgy and chemistry.

The accomplishments of Italian craftsmen, he felt, were limited by their inherited traditions. The methods used were inevitably the same, passed down for centuries from grandfather to father, from father to son. Many of his fellow countrymen believed that the old ideas were quite adequate, and they guarded their professional secrets in their families—secrets of certain qualities of ground-up bricks or special types of manure used for mixing in the core of their castings.

In many of the rare old bronzes, an expert eye or the use of a microscope may detect many faults. These faults of casting were often hidden by the clever craftsman. The early sculptors deemed it essential to learn this part of their profession and excelled in perfecting the last detail of their own bronze casts. The sculptor's studio used to include a melting oven and crucible and all the tools needed to mend or finish a bronze.

Where can we find this now? Today the sculptor turns over his plaster

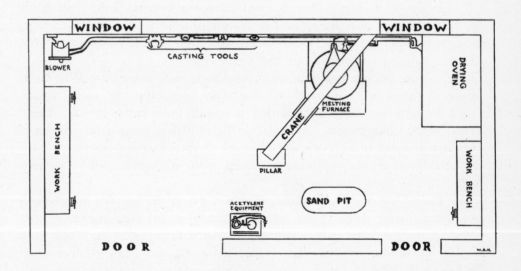

254. Small Bronze Foundry at the Stella Elkins Tyler Fine Arts School, Temple University, Showing Furnace for Melting Metal Set in the Floor. Crucible Suspended Above on a Crane; Compressed-air Fan on Left for Forcing Draft; Oven on the Right for Drying Sand Molds and Melting Wax. Ink Drawing by William Hildebrandt.

model to a foundry and demands a perfect bronze reproduction. He hardly ever interests himself in how this result is obtained or by whose hands the work is done. If the artists themselves have lost interest in the hows and wherefores of their work, it is small wonder that the general public, and even the art collectors, are in a sort of vague trance when it comes to understanding how a work of art in bronze is actually produced. They only keep on wondering sadly—why is sculpture so expensive?

The effect of efficient mass production by machinery has destroyed interest in and respect for master artisanship. It has forced the maker of art bronzes to compete with lower prices, and yet wages have risen in every branch of work. To develop this art and train expert workers in the face of such discouraging conditions has been a long, hard fight, but the fact is that today, in this country, there exist quite a number of good foundries which have sprung up since 1900 and whose head craftsmen were the pioneers who followed the first little group brought to America by Mr. Bertelli.

It is believed that even previous to the time of Benvenuto Cellini, the artist prepared a core of crushed brick or plaster, resembling the figure he intended to model, but slightly smaller in all its contours. On this he built up his wax figure. He now set a number of metal pins through the wax into the core. When he completed the surface modeling in the wax, he covered it entirely with a mixture of liquid plaster and clay. Additional coats were applied, being carefully built up without disturbing the first coat next to the wax. The metal pins projected through all these layers so that the core and coverings were all held together securely. When the mold had dried and hardened, it was heated in an oven of about 500°. This caused all the wax to melt and run out of a hole left in the bottom of the mold. The empty spaces left by this melted wax were actually the channels and forms into which the subsequent molten bronze was poured, and left to cool and harden, hence the name cire perdue, or lost wax. Then the outer layers of the mold were broken off and the core shaken out as thoroughly as possible and the bronze cleaned. (If the core is left in, it will absorb moisture and is likely to discolor or make spots on the finished bronze. In the case of lead casting, the wet core may cause the lead to crack and corrode in a serious, destructive manner.) The projecting pins were cut off and the surface chased to remove all roughness—a nice little job all by itself! The bronze was then ready to be patined or buffed and polished as desired.

When made in this manner, there is only one bronze, and this unique piece automatically destroys the original wax figure modeled by the sculptor. There is no plaster cast used in this process. In our day, the sculptor nearly always has his original work cast into plaster, and *this* is reproduced by the gelatine or plaster mold method, and cast into bronze by either the lost-wax or the sand process described later on.

Tin, copper, zinc, and aluminum or phosphorus, mixed in different proportions, give various qualities to the alloy known as bronze. For its greater strength, phosphor bronze is often used in machine castings. Manganese is also added for castings which are subjected to great friction.

If people are interested in the care and upkeep of bronzes in houses or museums, they might like to know that it is advisable to rub the bronzes thoroughly with a soft flannel cloth once a week. This will remove all soot and dust and keep the surface clean and lustrous. Care should be taken not to rub too hard or long, especially on the salient forms, such as noses, cheekbones, etc., but evenly on the entire surface, avoiding friction or pressure.

If a bronze has been neglected for a long time and is covered with accumulated dust, it is well to rub it over carefully with a soft, long-haired brush so that all the crevices and undercuts are cleaned out before the entire surface is rubbed with a flannel cloth. If a high polish is desired, a cloth or soft brush may be dipped into a can of soft floor wax or liquid wax and brushed lightly over the bronze and left to dry. After five or six hours this may be carefully rubbed and a high polish obtained. This treatment may also be given to bronzes left out of doors. The color of bronzes often changes when exposed to the elements, turning darker or in many instances into a dull black color. Some sculptors feel that the patine of green withstands the ravages of severe climate more successfully than the brown or golden tones. Another method of cleaning a bronze placed out of doors is to begin a few months after the placing by washing with hard soap and brushes and a little ammonia. When dry the surface should be rubbed with liquid wax, and the elements themselves will gradually create a good natural patine on the bronze. This should be done whenever the surface collects grime. If through neglect the bronze is too crusted with dirt and grime, it should be washed off with nitric, chloric, or oxalic acid and water until the original bronze surface is clean. Then this should be waxed and rubbed.

It is always wiser to consult a specialist before experimenting with acids of any kind. Great risks are taken when amateurs play with inflammable or poisonous fluids, and the bronzes are liable to accidental injury.

Many rare examples of ancient bronzes have been injured by malignant patine; this disease of metals sometimes remains a long time inactive and then shows signs at intervals of continuing its destructive work. (See illustration.)

Restoration of ancient bronzes is a most delicate operation, needing the direction of an expert. Extraordinary results have been achieved in many museums.

CIRE-PERDUE, OR LOST-WAX, PROCESS, AS USED TODAY

The first stage of this process consists in preparing a negative gelatine or plaster piece mold of the sculptor's original model.

In this negative mold, which shows all the details of the model in reverse, a wax coating is applied in a molten state with a brush until it has acquired sufficient thickness, depending on the size of the figure.

At this stage, we have a perfect replica of the sculpture in wax, and sufficiently hard to permit handling. The artist can work on it as much as he pleases, obtaining rare results of detail, which makes this process of casting invaluable. Wax rods for gates and air vents are then properly attached to the wax figure and lead from the cone-shaped entrance opening to all parts of the model. (See illustration.)

Finally, the mold for the metal is formed by blowing or pouring a core inside, and covering the outside of the wax with a semiliquid composition

255. Bronze Statuette of the Egyptian Goddess, Sekhmet, Before and After Treatment. Serious Corrosion Due to Malignant Patine Threatened to Destroy This Priceless Specimen. Treatment Not Only Eliminated the Malignant Matter but Exposed Much Delicate Detail. Field Museum of Natural History.

256. *Showing the First Coating of Finely Ground Material Over the Wax and the Second, Heavier Coating Which Completes the Mold in the Lost-wax Process. Projecting Pins Pierce Outer Mold, Wax, and Inner Core, Holding All in Place.*

which hardens in a few minutes. Pins are placed to hold all these layers in place, transpiercing core, wax, and mold.

Material used for core: one and one-half plaster to two parts of silica (or of silica and brick dust mixed). These materials are mixed with water until a smooth, creamy consistency is obtained. This same mixture is used, only slightly thicker in consistency, for covering the wax with the first coating. For outer layers on the mold, this same material may be applied in still rougher consistency.

After making the first bronze, the outside molds (which must be stronger than the inside ones) are ground up again; this material is mixed in the proportion of two parts to one and one-half of plaster, mixed with water. This is used many times, over and over, for the outer molds. The first coating over the wax, however, must always be new silica or brick dust and fine plaster, to assure a perfect reproduction of all details. For wax receipts see page 305.

The outer composition of silica, plaster, etc., is sometimes mixed with sawdust and charcoal and can resist high temperature (about 2300°). When heated, all the wax inside will melt away, leaving a hollow space between the core and the mold outside. This operation is accomplished in large ovens by baking the molds over a slow fire (about 1200°). As soon as all the wax

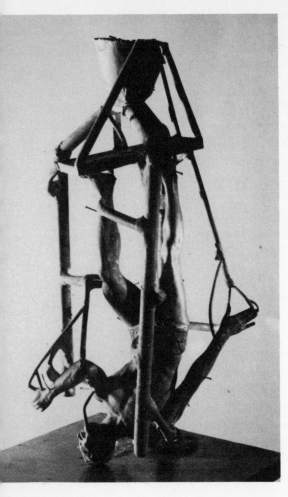

257, 258. Bronze Figure of "Liberian Dancer" by Malvina Hoffman. The Lost-wax Method of Casting This Figure Is Shown in Diagram. This Is the Way the Bronze Actually Appears When It Comes Out of the Mold. All the Metal Vents and Gates Must Be Removed and the Surface Cleaned. All Spaces Previously Filled by the Wax in the Mold Have Now Been Filled with Molten Bronze, and These Must Be Cut Off and the Surfaces Cleaned. The Inside of This Figure Is Hollow Because Originally the Wax Was Filled with a Core as Described in the Text.

.(L. MOHOLY-NAGY, 1938)

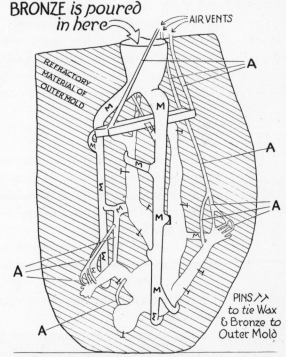

BRONZE is poured in here→

AIR VENTS

REFRACTORY MATERIAL OF OUTER MOLD

A

A

A

A

A

PINS ⋋⋋ to tie Wax & Bronze to Outer Mold

MOLD IS SET UPSIDE DOWN FOR POURING BRONZE —

M: Bronze-enters at funnel & rises from below

A: Air Vents which allow air to escape at the top. Otherwise Bronze would not rise to fill fingers & other details —

is melted away, the mold is removed from the oven and packed in foundry earth in a pit provided in the floor. The mold must not be allowed to cool off too much, as this would chill the metal as it enters and cause gaps in the bronze cast. The bronze is then poured from crucibles, and the molten metal runs through the gates and vents (wax having melted away) and fills the space left empty by the wax figure (also melted away), the air having escaped via the vents to allow the metal to rise freely to all parts. The figure in bronze is then removed from the outer mold and dipped in acid for a proper cleaning. The core is shaken out or picked out by wires.

With this process, the cast bronzes require very little finishing or chiseling, and the results are considered by some to be far above those obtained by the sand process.

The patining of the finished bronzes is an art in itself; the different effects of color are obtained by the use of different chemicals (see pages 302, 304).

Bronze is an alloy of from 85 to 90 per cent of copper, and from 10 to 15 per cent tin, zinc, and other nonferrous metals. The alloy, so-called United States Standard Bronze, is composed of 90 per cent copper, 7 per cent tin, and 3 per cent zinc. This formula is not by any means officially approved by the United States government; the name was given it by some bronze foundrymen only a few years ago, and, strange to say, it became official.

No one should be alarmed about the durability of bronze, as there are thousands of specimens all over the world in an admirable condition of preservation composed of every conceivable proportion of alloy.

SAND PROCESS

The sculptor's original plaster model is packed in fine "French sand," a composition of clay, silica, and alumina pressed snugly against every surface of the plaster model. This is encased in iron flasks (frames) strongly built in sections of perfect mechanical construction and held tightly together by clamps and bolts.

The molder gently hammers the damp sand against the plaster model, taking care of the undercuts, or deep recesses, by making as many sand pieces as necessary, in such a way as to be able to release them from the original model by taking them apart without injury either to them or to the model.

After the model is released, the packed sand pieces, which bear the impression of the most minute details of the original model, are recomposed in their iron frames and constitute the complete mold. A proper sand core is

259. Iron Bar for Carrying and Tipping Crucible.

260. Machine for Grinding Up Sand and Core Material.

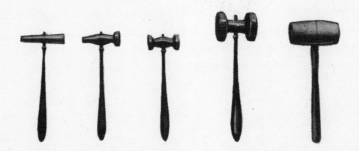

261. Types of Hammers and Mallets Used in Chasing and Finishing Metals.

262. *How the Founder Lifts the Cover from the Oven in Which the Molten Bronze Is Being Heated, Before Pouring Into the Mold. He Wears Apron, Mittens, and Leggings of Wet Carpet or Asbestos to Protect Himself from the Intense Heat and Flying Sparks.* (RUDIER FOUNDRY)

263. *Skimming Off the Molten Bronze While in the Tilting Furnace.*

(ROMAN BRONZE WORKS SPOT FILMS, INC.)

264. *Large Crucible Carried by Crane and Tilted by Two Men to Pour the Molten Metal Into the Mold. Note That the Plug Is Still Left in the Upper Reservoir.* (ROMAN BRONZE WORKS SPOT FILMS, INC.)

265. *After the Plug Is Removed the Molten Metal Flows Into the Mold and Overflows at the Top as a Signal That Every Part of the Mold Has Been Filled.*
(ROMAN BRONZE WORKS SPOT FILMS, INC.)

now built inside them. The surface of this core is then so shaved that it leaves a space between itself and the sand pieces above described, and is suspended by iron pins which go through it and the sand mold in many directions.

After this operation, the sand molds must be carefully dried in an oven properly built. When they have completely dried, the liquid bronze at about 1500° to 1900° F. is poured into the molds held in the iron flasks, previously clamped together; it runs through channels skillfully cut in the sand which direct and carry it into all the empty spaces between the core and the mold.

The sand is then removed and the core shaken out. After the bronze is cleaned with nitric acid, it will be finished and chiseled by expert artisans. This process is known as "chasing."

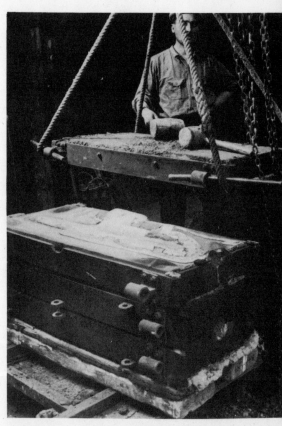

266. *Bronze Casting (Sand Process) of a Bull Fighting a Bear. The Inlets for the Liquid Metal Carry the Bronze to All the Sections of the Mold and Underneath the Base, so that the Flow of the Metal Is Kept in Equalized Quantities all Over the Subject. The Mold Is Always Set Upside Down and the Metal Poured in Through the Top.*

(RUDIER FOUNDRY)

267. *The Sectional Metal Frames Used in Sand Process of Bronze Casting. These Are All Set Together and Bolted Firmly to Prevent Any Movement or Shifting When the Molten Metal Is Poured Into the Mold.*

(RUDIER FOUNDRY)

268. *An Electric Machine Drilling Holes for the Bolts Which Hold the Sections Together.* (RUDIER FOUNDRY)

269. *Welding Two Sections of a Bronze Cast Together with a Compressed-air Blowtorch.* (RUDIER FOUNDRY)

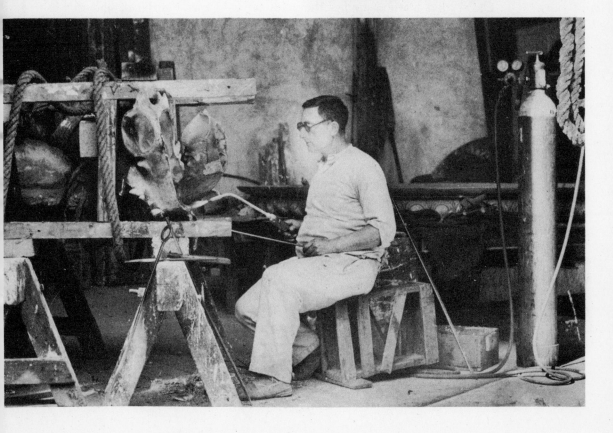

BRONZE PATINING

Il faut attraper les accidents et les convertir en science.*

(RODIN TO M. H., PARIS, 1910)

The subject of patining is almost impossible to treat with scientific exactness. Even if careful receipts and proportions of solutions are followed, the results will always depend upon the individual who applies these chemicals to the surface of the bronze, brass, or silver. The best way is to study the subject with an expert and make your own experiments under his guidance, until you achieve good results. Watch for accidental effects, and learn to stop in time, when you happen to get a suitable or handsome color.

There are two methods of patining bronze. One necessitates the heating of the surface by a blowtorch held in the left hand, while the right hand holds the brush and dips this frequently into the bowls of acids and applies them to the heated bronze. At intervals the bronze is washed off in cold water to prevent too thick an application of acids. The heat opens the pores to receive the acid; the water checks it in the same manner as tempering carving tools.

The second method applies the acids on cold metal surfaces, and this is often preferable for large figures that are to be left out of doors.

Copper is a metal which tarnishes quickly in damp air, and develops a film of blackish or brownish color in time. Green deposits of a basic carbonate of copper are often formed on this metal; this is erroneously often called verdigris.

RECEIPTS FOR PATINING BRONZE (90% COPPER, 7% TIN, 3% ZINC)

Yellowish green: Color is obtained by using a solution of

Ammonium chloride	3½	lbs.
Copper acetate	2	lbs.
Water	1	gal.

Apple green:

Sodium chloride	20	oz.
Ammonia	16	fluid oz.
Ammonium chloride	20	oz.
Vinegar	1	gal.

* Catch the accidents, and convert them into science.

270. *Père and Jean Limet, "Master Patineurs," in Their Paris Studio, 1938.*
Blowtorch Heating the Bronze Before Applying Acids with Brush.

(PHOTO BY M. H.)

Bluish green:	Sodium thiosulphate	1	oz.
	Nitrate of iron	8	oz.
	Water	1	gal.

Antique green:	Copper sulphate	12	oz.
	Ammonium chloride	2	oz.
	Water	1	gal.
	Rinse in cold, then hot water.		

Shades of brown:	Potassium sulphide	2	oz.
	Barium sulphide	4	oz.
	Ammonia	8	fluid oz.
	Water	3 to 5	gals.

Antique effect: Wash the bronze over with nitrate of copper. Let it dry. Add a thick coating of nitrate of copper. Stipple over with sal ammoniac and pulverized modeling clay. Add a little powdered chalk. Atomize entire surface with milk. Let this dry, and colors will be set.

Renaissance black: Cover bronze with nitrate of copper and let it oxidize and dry a bit. Heat surface lightly over smoking straw fire, until desired color is obtained. Keep turning the bronze in the smoke. Clean surface with chloride of ammonia. Bury in flower pot of sand. Pour milk into this to soaking point every two days. After two weeks take out bronze, cover it with chalk, and rebury in the sand; pour milk in every two days for two or three weeks. Take out and brush off surface.

Oxidation of silver: 3 drams potassium sulphide in 1 gallon of water, solution at 160° F. A silver coin touching India rubber will become oxidized, when sulphur has been used to vulcanize the rubber. Ammonium sulphide 40 fluid ounces, water 1 gallon, gives good oxidation. A high polish may be obtained by rubbing on a mixture of beeswax and turpentine; sometimes a drop of olive oil may be added. Sometimes the high lights on figures or metal reliefs need polishing. This is done by carefully burnishing the surface. If a dull finish is needed, sandblasting may be used. Great care must be taken, however, in both these cases, not to injure the effect of the modeling.

If a dull black is desired on brass (as in lining of telescope tubes, etc.), use bismuth nitrate, dissolved in water.

AVERAGE INGREDIENTS OF WAX FOR BRONZE CASTINGS

1. Pure yellow beeswax .... 1 lb.
   Turpentine of Venice .... 4 oz.

2. Pure yellow beeswax .... 1.3 ⎫
   Pure bleached wax (white) .... 0.1 ⎬ = 2 kilogs.
   Paraffin .... 0.4 ⎪
   (Colophane) resin .... 0.2 ⎭

3. Pure yellow beeswax .... 10 grams
   (Colophane) resin .... 10 "
   Carbonate of lime .... 90 "
   Olive oil .... 90 "

Each one of these compounds can be colored either with green or red stearate or with English vermilion. Add until the wax is colored to the shade desired.

Melt the wax and then add coloring matter. Stir well.

In order to melt the wax and prevent it from burning or taking fire, put the pot containing the wax on a very low fire. Some people melt the wax in a double boiler. This is a good idea. In case a double boiler cannot be secured, a sheet of asbestos is put between the flame and the pot. *Great care* must be taken not to allow a drop of turpentine to splash into the flame.

In my own experience I have found that compound No. 1 is the best, and the formula given is in general correct, but sometimes according to the quality of the wax the proportion of the turpentine of Venice has to be changed. After the wax has been melted, wait until it cools and then see if the consistency is good. If not, add a little more turpentine of Venice and melt again. In order to determine when the wax is ready for use, allow a little of it to cool, and rub it between your fingers and thumb. It should have a very fine plastic quality.

CLEANING METAL

Metal that has become very dirty and discolored with rust may be washed with brown American potash, one-half to one pound in one gallon of water heated in an iron pot. The metal may be immersed and soaked before scouring with a cotton mop. Aluminum and zinc must only be dipped in the solution, not left there, as they would dissolve.

If heavily coated with grease, the metal must be wiped with benzine
gasoline on a cotton cloth, dried, and then scoured with the hot pota
solution. *Do not smoke* during any of these operations when inflammab
materials are being used. Be careful, also, to cork all containers immediate
after using their contents, such as benzine, alcohol, gasoline, turpentin
shellac, etc.

HARD SOLDERING

To remove all dirt and oxide a flux compound of zinc chloride, sal a
moniac, and tin is applied to the surface to be soldered and left for fi
minutes, after which time zinc, brass, and copper may be soldered at a hi
temperature.

SOFT SOLDERING

Powdered resin, often mixed with sal ammoniac, or resin alone, may
applied to the cleaned parts to be soldered with lead or tin. Solder will adhe
only to the parts covered by this flux.

Silver solder is used for jewelry and may be heated to high temperatu
The flux used for this is borax.

The soldering iron is made of an iron shaft set in a wooden handle; t
tip is riveted to a pyramidal head of copper. This tip should be wiped w
tow before using. It is heated to a dull red color, rubbed with sal ammoni
and then held against the solder.

If you sweat (heat) two metal surfaces for soldering, be sure you do n
overheat the metal to be soldered, or it will melt before the solder does a
your job will be spoiled. One should be sure of the relative fusing points
the metals and solders used.

BRAZING SILVER, BRASS, COPPER, OR OTHER HARI METALS

Clean parts to be joined and set end to end on fire bricks. Refracto
material (crushed asbestos or sand) may be packed around these. Wa
metal ends with borax paste kept near in a bowl. Heat ends to be joine
white hot, by a blowtorch blue flame. Hold brass or solder over hot en
It will melt and run along the joint. Let it all cool and set. File off exc
brass or solder.

OTHER TREATMENTS OF METAL

Iron may be heated and welded together by hammering on an anvil only; it is used for its strength and endurance as well as for its decorative, rugged qualities for gates, grills, etc.

A fractional amount of carbon added to iron converts it into steel. Prehistoric man found out how to make iron weapons from meteoric metals, for by analysis it has been found that the earliest iron weapons have in them an alloy of nickel, a combination found only in meteoric specimens.

Before the casting of liquid metals, early repoussé metalwork was done on thin sheets of bronze or brass hammered on a wooden core. Later the metal was put over a bed of pitch and pounded brick and the design hammered into relief from the back. The bed of pitch prevented holes being punched through the metal and yielded sufficiently to the reliefs to act as a negative mold. When finished, the pitch was melted off, and if finishing touches were needed on the positive face of the relief the pitch was applied to the back and the same process was followed for the front of the relief.

The Siris bronzes of the fourth century B.C. in the British Museum are amazing examples of this kind of repoussé work in high relief, almost in the round, and yet with unbroken surfaces of paper-thin bronze.

Byzantine artists excelled in all forms of metalwork and kept this art alive when the fall of the Roman Empire destroyed the fine arts in almost all other areas. Later on, Byzantium handed on its torch of art to Roman and Florentine artists in the sixth and eighth centuries, as well as to the Rhine provinces during the Middle Ages, until the magnificent Renaissance of the fifteenth century brought art again into its full flowering and brilliant epoch.

ELECTRODEPOSITION OF METAL

On base metals, such as iron, tin, zinc, and lead, a thin surface of copper, silver, nickel, or gold may be applied evenly and colored with acids to give the desired effect.

In lead-lined, wooden vats containing acid cyanide solutions (which are good conductors), *anodes* (flat pieces of the metal, such as copper or brass) are hung on a rod of metal, which is connected to the positive terminal of an electric generator. The current enters the solution by way of the anode and dissolves it. From another rod the work to be plated is hung. This is a *cathode*. It is connected to the negative electric terminal and receives the

271. "The Chariot of Apollo," Versailles. When the Pool Is Filled with Water All the Pipes Are Covered, Giving the Illusion That the Horses Are Swimming in the Water; the Jets Spray the Foam Ahead of Them. All These Lead Sculptures Were Removed, Cleaned, and Rearmatured, and Where the Forms Had Cracked or Given Way They Were Hammered Back Into Their Original Shapes.

(RUDIER FOUNDRY)

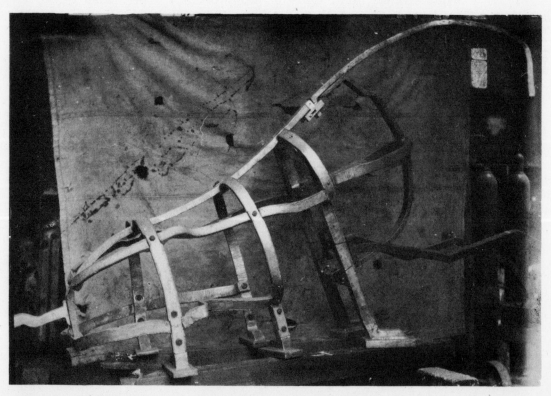

272. Internal Iron Framework, Hermetically Covered by Hand-hammered Lead Before Being Reset Inside the Lead Horses of Apollo. (RUDIER FOUNDRY)

deposited metal. The current passes through a rheostat to control and regulate the amount used.

Into the vats the following acids are poured: copper sulphate, ammonia, and potassium cyanide (or sulphuric acid) dissolved in strong solutions. There are many variations and degrees of mixtures, depending on the metals and results required. Sometimes warm solutions are used, sometimes cold.

The cathodes must be absolutely clean before being plated.

ELECTROPLATING PLASTER

Galvano Process

The plaster must first be warmed and thoroughly dried. It is then soaked in linseed oil for half an hour. (Some prefer soaking in wax instead of oil.) When all excess oil has drained off, it is dried again in an oven of 160° F. The surface must have a continuous skin of hard oil entirely covering every part of the model. If any portion remains porous, the plating solution will enter the pores and ruin the model. If necessary, the oiling process must be repeated two or three times. Then rub the entire surface with fine graphite and a brush and immerse it in the acid bath as described in the section on medals.

SILVER PLATING

Wash the plaster model with a solution of silver nitrate and alcohol, and leave it to dry. Then put the model in a hermetically sealed container, into which a jet of sulphureted hydrogen is passed. This gas, coming into contact with the silver nitrate, turns it into silver sulphide.

Rinse and wash well. Attach wires to many points of the model, if possible in hidden places where points of contact will not be too evident.

Another method is to coat the surface with orange shellac and alcohol and Venetian turpentine. When still sticky, brush on a coat of fine copper bronze powder and attach the wires as before described. The model is now sunk in the plating bath, and the current turned on. A good imitation of bronze is obtained in this manner.

Wood may be varnished or oiled, as in the case of plaster, and then be metal plated in the same manner as described above.

The galvano results are exact and accurate reproductions of the original model.

273. "The Faun," by Paul Dardé, Cast in Lead by the Rudier Foundry, Showing Method by Which a Colossal Figure Is Loaded onto a Truck.

274. "The Gate of Hell," by Rodin. Colossal Bronze Cast Placed in the Garden of the Rodin Museum, Paris. (RUDIER FOUNDRY)

275. *"Hippocrates," on the Medical and Public Health Build-ing, New York World's Fair, 1939, Made from Different Metals to Achieve a Variety of Color. Designed by Hildreth Meière, Executed by the Rambusch Metal Shop.*

(COPYRIGHT, THE NEW YORK WORLD'S FAIR, 1939, INC.)

276. *"Brass Toy," by Gaudier-Brzeska.*

(FROM "THE MEANING OF MODERN SCULPTURE," BY R. H. WILENSKI)

XVIII. Originals or Fakes?

WHAT is an "original"? This question might well be asked concerning the great number of replicas which have been made of the most popular subjects by well-known sculptors of many countries. For these clever replicas in plaster, terra cotta, and stone are often so exactly like the original that even accredited experts are deceived. The same situation applies to the extraordinary marble copies of old masters which have flooded the market recently.

It is, of course, much more difficult to make a marble copy good enough to deceive experts than merely to squeeze out another clay from the original mold, retouch it, and bake it in an oven. For "terra cotta" means "baked clay," and the varied tones of pink and tan may be determined either by the quality of the clay used to press out the copy from a plaster negative mold, or by applying the desired color afterwards. Fakes are often buried in the ground or sand or ashes for a long enough time to discolor the surface, and give the new baked clay the appearance of "really old antique," as we are often assured in the shops.

Some years ago I was asked to appear as a witness for an art dealer who had imported three pieces of sculpture from Paris: a marble, a bronze, and a terra cotta head. The customhouse raised the question of what constituted an actual original. (In this special case the question referred to a living sculptor.)

The art dealer, knowing that I was familiar with the methods and signature of this particular artist, asked me to describe briefly the differences between the original clay sketch, the first plaster cast, the first bronze, and the terra cotta original.

It may surprise the reader, as it certainly did some of the listeners at the customhouse, to find that actually the only material which should be called "original" is the clay or plasteline model actually made by the sculptor's hand. This model, however, is nearly always completely destroyed when the first plaster waste mold is made, except in the case of a terra cotta, when it is the original potter's clay pressed into a negative mold and then baked that constitutes the finished product.

Of course if this negative mold is preserved, as it frequently is, any number of replicas may be pressed into it and baked. They will be identical in appearance unless the sculptor works over each replica with variations, but the first one is generally considered the legitimate original. In the case under discussion, I called the attention of the examiners to the thumbprints clearly visible on the inside of the terra cotta. (This sculptor would often press his thumb into the clay and, smiling, would say, "This is the only real signature of a sculptor.") They were able to verify this imprint with many others which were visible on his original clay studies.

It is quite often possible to find the reproduction of an artist's fingerprint in a first plaster cast or even in certain bronzes. If an impression of the sculptor's thumb could be registered in wax, it might prove helpful in doubtful cases of identification.

To explain the bronze process, I described how after the clay is destroyed and the plaster cast made, the next step is to make a negative gelatine mold on this plaster. This gelatine, in turn, is lined with a thin layer of wax, which is filled inside with a core of liquid material which hardens. A thick outside covering of refractory material on the wax completes the mold. When all these materials, now in a solid mass, are baked, the wax runs out and leaves the empty space between core and outside covering. This space (about one-eighth of an inch in small sculpture) is filled with the molten bronze. When this cools, the outer shell is broken off and the core shaken out, and the bronze emerges covered with metal jets, vents, and pins attached to its surface. These must be carefully removed by an expert chaser (surface finisher). Then the bronze is cleaned and patined and the work is completed.

The first bronze is generally numbered 1, and is called the original; in many cases of small figures or groups an edition is limited to a very few copies, then the mold is broken by the sculptor. The bronze under discussion was a number 1, and therefore was admitted by the customs authorities without duty.

In the case of identifying a marble, the title of "original" becomes even more complicated. For in many cases sculptors do not touch their marbles, but have them pointed up from the plaster model and finished by expert carvers. If the sculptor has learned how to carve, he should take over the work when the rough pointing is finished and carry on the work to the end himself. It was found possible to prove the authenticity of the marble in question, because the sculptor had finished the work himself in his own special manner and easily identified technique.

One can guess that by the time all these processes were explained, the listeners were glad to take a sculptor's word for it. The three pieces were passed as originals, and everybody was glad to declare a recess and go out to lunch!

In the case of a theft of a copyrighted piece, it is very difficult for a sculptor to trace his bronze or have any protection from future counterfeits being sold. False bronzes are slightly smaller in size than the authentic original, but otherwise similar. This difference in size is sometimes a clue in tracing a suspicious copy; another clue is the quality of surface texture, and detail, which gradually loses its crispness. Every metal casting shrinks about one-sixteenth of an inch to one foot.

I recall with amusement the excursion that I arranged for one of my friends whose house is graced by many authentic works of art, including work by the sculptor Houdon. I asked her if she would care to see a collection of Houdons in terra cotta and plaster. When she reached Paris, I drove her to a faraway street, on the left bank, and pushed open a little wooden door in a high wall. "Which subject would you like to see first," I asked, "for I feel sure Monsieur can show you almost anything you may choose."

We entered the large studio; the walls were lined with shelves, and these in turn were laden with Houdons, Carpeaux, Pigalles, and Clodions of every shape and variety. Seeing a veritable factory of sculpture was rather a shock to my friend, especially as she saw the "antique" copies of the subjects in her own collection being carefully wrapped up for shipment to America.

There was no secrecy whatever in this factory. It is a flourishing and well-known business in many countries, and only becomes dangerous when used by unscrupulous dealers, who purchase a copy for 150 francs, and then by treating its surface, adding perhaps a seal or a signature, and cultivating a market for this particular object, resell the copy to unsuspecting clients as a "bona fide" original, pedigree included, for thousands of dollars.

It is not an easy game, this faking of old sculpture, and often the dealer has to wait five or ten years before pretending to discover his own "antique." It takes years to create a market, and until there is a demand he knows he cannot make his profit.

The client needs the artist, the artist needs his public, the dealer needs both, and both depend upon the dealer for more than they can estimate. Were it not for dealers and galleries, many good artists would never be discovered or made famous. Collectors and clients are usually shy of visiting artists in their studios; the latter must rely on selling their work through reliable agents or galleries, where the art of selling is better understood and enjoyed by all parties concerned.

The artistic history of a race is lastingly recorded in stone carvings and paintings. When buildings have been destroyed and books burned, the only traces of a lost civilization are found painted and graven upon rocks or carved in marble. Dealers knowing the values of these treasures invest in them, and it is a long wait before they find their buyers. They risk their capital for a future market, relying on their own judgment and ability.

So let us be hopeful and confident that in spite of false Rodins and Houdons, and the talented Dossena's recent contribution of a remarkable series of copies of "old masters," we can all continue to work with the knowledge that "Tho old the thought and oft expressed, 'tis his at last who says it best."

The fact that the game of collecting is a risky one only adds interest and adventure for the modern buyer. It challenges him to train his eye and mind to a keener perception of art, and this automatically contributes joy and satisfaction—both to himself and to his contemporary artists.

In the famous studio of Houdon, many replicas of his expressive portraits were cast in plaster under his direction, and marked with his seal. In a letter to one of his clients, he wrote asking the lady if he might reserve the right of making thirty replicas of her portrait. If during his lifetime so many copies were authorized by the sculptor himself, is it any wonder that since his death, with a constantly growing appreciation of and demand for his work, the numbers of Houdons have multiplied so that it would be impossible to trace the authenticity of all those which are sold and distributed as genuine? The game of collecting is one which will test your own sense of humor if you are fooled, and your ability and artistic taste if you have acquired a genuine work of art. For this is an asset which, like good wine, grows better with age.

There is a sort of honest graft that you must not begrudge to those who are cleverer than you are. It should challenge and stimulate you to study the subject thoroughly. It is easier to buy than to sell a work of art these days. The artist cannot live without the necessities of life; a beefsteak is just as good for a poor painter or sculptor in an attic as it is for the banker—perhaps even better, only it is more difficult for the artist to procure one. The idea that good art flourishes only when its creator is starving is a worn-out fallacy. The real gamble, it seems to me, in spite of inevitable disappointments, would be to endow a living human being of talent and ability, to enable him to create his brain children without the mental torture of paying rent and food bills from the sale of his art—until he "arrives"! Instead of this, the safer and more usual form of philanthropy is to endow a bed in a hospital, in which a man may suffer and die, or, if he is lucky, be brought back to fighting form to continue his struggles against still greater obstacles.

It is obviously less of a risk to buy antiques and the work of men who have passed the test of time; but in the good old days, if the art patrons had not had the courage and imagination to stimulate their own contemporary artists to heroic efforts, and be their moral as well as financial backers, where would we turn for many of our inspirations and museum collections today?

The artist, being a highly sensitive human being, is much affected by the attitude of his public, whether he is willing to acknowledge this fact or not. When a creative mind feels that there is a responsive understanding or need of its work, it is automatically stimulated and encouraged. The fact that a creator feels his work to be of essential value to someone for whom he has respect, that he is believed in and expected to produce better and better results, is a great moral stimulus. Creative activity generates new energy and strength; it means re-creation in its true sense.

When the recent financial crash struck our country, the stratum of society which was affected immediately and lastingly was the art world. When people stop building houses, architects and builders face bankruptcy. When architects and their clients cease to engage decorators, mural painters, and sculptors, this whole imaginative world is faced with a staggering situation. Art becomes "de luxe" and is therefore branded as unnecessary. Even music is considered a luxury by those who do not realize that its magic influence may uplift us and give us new hope. It may take a long time for a country to realize the actual value of its art production, but gradually the sense of loss in this field of the spirit has to be reckoned with. "Where there is no vision, the people perish." Perhaps suffering and despair have to be experienced before a new era of beauty may come to life, before there can be a renaissance. There must be fire and ashes before the phoenix may rise from them!

L'Envoi

AS this book on *Sculpture* comes to an end, I am more convinced than ever of what I have always suspected. There is really little to say, and no need to explain a work of art.

But I have been asked to write about sculpture in such a way that the pages might be of use to serious students, and of interest to the general public. This opportunity has given a sort of winged freedom to my thoughts. If my book can be a friendly companion to other wayfarers, if by my own errors and experience it is possible for me to warn them of the dangerous places, I am willing to risk the judgment of all the other readers.

Honestly, it has not been possible for me to be conscious of either while writing. I only jotted down what impressed me as guideposts during the journey. It is easier to lay down a rule than to obey it, and far easier to tell how sculpture should be done than to do it. I am in the grips of this plastic battle myself, forever searching to find the way in the wonderland of art. When a serious artist reviews the long records of the centuries, and sees the youth of today laying its foundations, he must of necessity be overwhelmed by the mass of material encompassed by this simple heading "sculpture."

Were it not for the fact that an amazing number of letters from students have asked me for professional advice since the publication of my book *Heads and Tales* two years ago, I should never have embarked on this volume.

This effort has brought me to my knees before the inevitable mystery. I can lift little more than a corner of the veil, but I've tried, and in so doing hope the result may not be entirely useless. I feel rather exhausted, and very, *very* small. How wonderful if now there could be found a quiet place on this globe where one might work uninterruptedly and carry out some of the new

ideas that have been striving to be born during the past few months—if one
might realize the vision that was Rilke's when he wrote:

> *And you wait, are awaiting the one thing*
> *that will infinitely increase your life;*
> *the powerful, the uncommon,*
> *the awakening of stones,*
> *depths turned towards you.*
>
> .   .   .   .   .
>
> *And you know all at once: That was it.*
> *You arise, and before you stands*
> *a bygone year's*
> *anguish and form and prayer.*

Translations from the Poetry of Rainer Maria Rilke
by M. D. HERTER NORTON

Index

Books That Live

The Norton imprint on a
book means that in the
publisher's estimation it
is a book not for a single
season but for the years.

W · W · NORTON & CO · INC.
70 FIFTH AVENUE
NEW YORK